1 Timothy

God's Plan for His Church

Every Body has a spiritual Gift

JOHN A. STEWART

© 2017 by LAMPLIGHTERS INTERNATIONAL

All rights reserved worldwide. International copyright secured. Unauthorized reproduction, distribution or storage, manually or electronically, of these materials in any form without the written consent of the author and the publisher is strictly prohibited.

Unless otherwise noted, all Scripture quotations are taken from the *New King James Version*, copyright 1982 by Thomas Nelson Inc. Used by permission. All rights reserved. Scripture quotations marked (NIV) are from the *Holy Bible, New International Version* (NIV), copyright 1973, 1978, 1984, 2011 by Biblica, Inc. Used by permission. All rights reserved. Scripture quotations marked (NLT) are taken from the *Holy Bible, New Living Translation*, copyright 1996. Used by permission of Tyndale House Publishers, Inc., Wheaton, IL. Used by permission. All rights reserved. Scripture quotations marked (Phillips) are from *The New Testament in Modern English* by J.B. Phillips, Copyright 1960, 1972 by J. B. Phillips. Administered by The Archbishops' Council of the Church of England. Used by permission. All rights reserved.

Lamplighters International is a Christian ministry that helps individuals engage with God and His Word and equips believers to be disciple-makers.

For additional information about Lamplighters ministry resources, contact:

Lamplighters International
771 NE Harding Street, Suite 250
Minneapolis, MN USA 55413
or visit our website at
www.LamplightersUSA.org.

Product Code 1Ti-NK-2P

ISBN 978-1-931372-68-8

Contents

"Character" = Actions in life
is
the only Value
Follow Christs example

How to Use This Study

What Is Lamplighters?

Lamplighters is a Christian ministry that helps individuals engage with God and His Word and equips believers to be disciple-makers. This Bible study, comprising ten individual lessons, is a self-contained unit and an integral part of the entire discipleship ministry. When you have completed the study, you will have a much greater understanding of a portion of God's Word, with many new truths that you can apply to your life.

How to study a Lamplighters Lesson

A Lamplighters study begins with prayer, your Bible, the weekly lesson, and a sincere desire to learn more about God's Word. The questions are presented in a progressive sequence as you work through the study material. You should not use Bible commentaries or other reference books (except a dictionary) until you have completed your weekly lesson and met with your weekly group. Approaching the Bible study in this way allows you to personally encounter many valuable spiritual truths from the Word of God.

To gain the most out of the Bible study, find a quiet place to complete your weekly lesson. Each lesson will take approximately 45–60 minutes to complete. You will likely spend more time on the first few lessons until you are familiar with the format, and our prayer is that each week will bring the discovery of important life principles.

The writing space within the weekly studies provides the opportunity for you to answer questions and respond to what you have learned. Putting answers in your own words, and including Scripture references where appropriate, will help you personalize and commit to memory the truths you have learned. The answers to the questions will be found in the Scripture references at the end of each question or in the passages listed at the beginning of each lesson.

If you are part of a small group, it's a good idea to record the specific dates that you'll be meeting to do the individual lessons. Record the specific dates each time the group will be meeting next to the lesson titles on the Contents page. Additional lines have been provided for you to record when you go through this same study at a later date.

The side margins in the lessons can be used for the spiritual insights you glean from other group or class members. Recording these spiritual truths will likely be a spiritual help to you and others when you go through this study again in the future.

Audio Introduction

A brief audio introduction is available to help you learn about the historical background of the book, gain an understanding of its theme and structure, and be introduced to some of the major truths. Audio introductions are available for all Lamplighters studies and are a great resource for the group leader; they can also be used to introduce the study to your group. To access the audio introductions, go to www.LamplightersUSA.org.

"*Do You Think?*" Questions

Each weekly study has a few *"do you think?"* questions designed to help you to make personal applications from the biblical truths you are learning. In the first lesson the *"do you think?"* questions are placed in italic print for easy identification. If you are part of a study group, your insightful answers to these questions could be a great source of spiritual encouragement to others.

Personal Questions

Occasionally you'll be asked to respond to personal questions. If you are part of a study group you may choose not to share your answers to these questions with the others. However, be sure to answer them for your own benefit because they will help you compare your present level of spiritual maturity to the biblical principles presented in the lesson.

A Final Word

Throughout this study the masculine pronouns are frequently used in the generic sense to avoid awkward sentence construction. When the pronouns *he*, *him*, and *his* are used in reference to the Trinity (God the Father, Jesus Christ, and the Holy Spirit), they always refer to the masculine gender.

This Lamplighters study was written after many hours of careful preparation. It is our prayer that it will help you "... grow in the grace and knowledge of our Lord and Savior Jesus Christ. To Him be the glory both now and forever. Amen" (2 Peter 3:18).

What Is an Intentional Discipleship Bible Study?

The *Next Step* in Bible Study

The Lamplighters Bible study series is ideal for individual, small group, and classroom use. This Bible study is also designed for Intentional Discipleship training. An Intentional Discipleship (ID) Bible study has four key components. Individually they are not unique, but together they form the powerful core of the ID Bible study process.

1. Objective: Lamplighters is a discipleship training ministry that has a dual objective: (1) to help individuals engage with God and His Word and (2) to equip believers to be disciple-makers. The small group format provides extensive opportunity for ministry training, and it's not limited by facilities, finances, or a lack of leadership staffing.

2. Content: The Bible is the focus rather than Christian books. Answers to the study questions are included within the study guides, so the theology is in the study material, not in the leader's mind. This accomplishes two key objectives: (1) It gives the group leader confidence to lead another individual or small group without fear, and (2) it protects the small group from theological error.

3. Process: The ID Bible study process begins with an Open House, which is followed by a 6–14-week study, which is followed by a presentation of the Final Exam (see graphic on page 8). This process provides a natural environment for continuous spiritual growth and leadership development.

4. Leadership Development: As group participants grow in Christ, they naturally invite others to the groups. The leader-trainer (1) identifies and recruits new potential leaders from within the group, (2) helps them register for online discipleship training, and (3) provides in-class leadership mentoring until they are both competent and confident to lead a group according to the ID Bible study process. This leadership development process is scalable, progressive, and comprehensive.

Overview of the Leadership Training and Development Process

There are three stages of leadership training in the Intentional Discipleship process: (1) leading studies, (2) training leaders, and (3) multiplying groups (see appendix for greater detail).

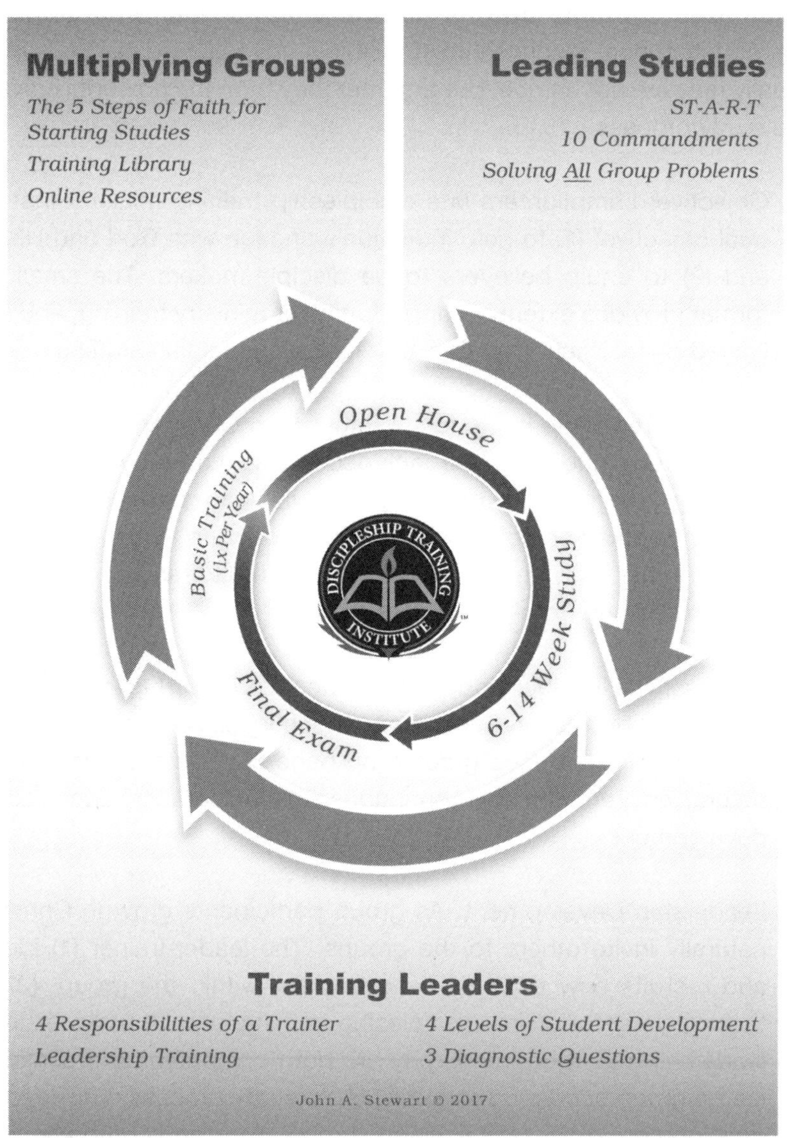

How Can I Be Trained?

Included within this Bible study is the student workbook for Level 1 (Basic Training). Level 1 training is both free and optional. Level 1 training teaches you a simple 4-step process (ST-A-R-T) to help you prepare a life-changing Bible study and 10 proven small group leadership principles that will help your group thrive. To register for a Level 1 online training event, either as an individual or as a small group, go to www.LamplightersUSA.org/training or www.discipleUSA.org. If you have additional questions, you can also call 800-507-9516.

ONE

STICK TO THE WORD

Read 1 Timothy 1:1–7; other references as given.

The books of 1 and 2 Timothy and Titus are commonly known as the Pastoral Epistles because they were written under the inspiration of the Holy Spirit to pastors (elders, overseers) of local churches. They provide Christians with a treasury of biblical instruction regarding (1) the effective administration of a local church and (2) how Christians should relate to one another within an assembly of faith.

No church or Christian can truly honor God and be effective in Christian ministry without a resolute commitment to the authority of God's Word. In this first lesson the apostle Paul commands Timothy, a pastor at Ephesus (an ancient city located in what is now western Turkey), to stick to the Word. The command is clear, and the consequences of not following Paul's exhortation are also clear. And the application to the church and every believer is patently obvious—stick to the Word.

Now ask God to reveal Himself through His Word and give you the grace to accept what you will be learning.

Lombardi Time Rule:

If the leader arrives early, he or she has time to pray, prepare the room, and greet others personally.

ADD GROUP INSIGHTS BELOW

1. No book in the Bible has a more clearly stated purpose for being written. Why did God direct the apostle Paul to write this letter to Timothy (1 Timothy 3:15)?

____

____

ADDITIONAL INSIGHTS

2. Paul refers to Timothy as his **true son** (1 Timothy 1:2) even though Timothy's biological father was an unsaved Gentile (Acts 16:1-3). What *do you think* Paul meant when he referred to Timothy as his son (Philippians 2:19–22)?

3. The phrase **grace, mercy, and peace** is a slight adaptation of an early Christian greeting that was often used by believers. It is, however, more than that. Grace is the sole basis upon which all God's gifts are bestowed upon man, mercy is the basis upon which God's holy wrath toward man is satisfied or assuaged, and peace is the result of being properly related to a righteous and loving God.

   a. What is the source of all three gifts?

   b. Take a moment to reflect upon your relationship with God.
      Are you trusting entirely in God's *grace* for eternal life?
      YES / NO / NOT SURE
      Are you grateful for God's *mercy* in your life?
      YES / NO
      Are you at *peace* with God?
      YES / NO / NOT REALLY

4. The book of Acts concludes with the apostle Paul imprisoned in Rome (Acts 28:16, 20, 30). Many Bible scholars believe Paul was eventually released and continued his missionary work before he was recaptured and beheaded in Rome.

During this interim period God used him to write two pastoral epistles to Timothy (1 and 2 Timothy) and one to Titus (Titus). Before Paul left Timothy at Ephesus and departed for Macedonia, what specific instructions did he give him (1 Timothy 1:3–4)?

1. ______________________________

____

2. ______________________________

____

Zip-It Rule:

Group members should agree to disagree, but should never be disagreeable.

ADDITIONAL INSIGHTS

5. If Timothy allowed these men to continue teaching their false doctrines in the church, what would be two negative results?

1. ______________________________

____

2. ______________________________

____

6. Many of God's people are confused about the primary purpose of the church's teaching ministry. Some believe the primary purpose of the public presentation of the Word is the salvation of the lost. Others believe the goal is the systematic presentation of truth so that God's people might gain a better knowledge of the Bible. Others believe that the purpose of biblical instruction is merely to encourage the saints. Still others believe the goal of biblical instruction is primarily social reform—the proclamation of moral and ethical ideals so that God's people might be salt and light in a corrupt world.

   a. What is the purpose of all biblical instruction (1 Timothy 1:5)? Please be complete with your answer.

____

____

ADDITIONAL INSIGHTS

____

____

b. What three things must be present in a believer's life before there can be a consistent manifestation of godly love?

1. ______________________________

2. ______________________________

3. ______________________________

7. Christians can become disillusioned when they realize there are false teachers within the body of Christ. Some believers even become cynical and develop a critical spirit toward all teachers of the Word. What word or phrase did Paul use to assure Timothy (and us as well) that not all religious teachers are "wolves in sheep's clothing" (1 Timothy 1:6)?

____

8. It is significant that the first chapter of 1 Timothy begins with the need for correct doctrine or theology within the church. It has been said that a church that is careless with its doctrine will be corrupt in its daily living. A lack of emphasis on the Scriptures in the church is not only shortsighted—it is a dangerous omission that will inevitably lead to heresy and apostasy. Why weren't the false teachers in the Ephesian church able to interpret the Scriptures correctly (1 Timothy 1:3–7)?

____

____

____

____

____

____

9. Throughout the history of the church false teaching has been the source of innumerable problems. There are at least three reasons why these false teachers would likely have been able to gain the spiritual confidence of the Christians at Ephesus. What are they (Galatians 3:1–3)?

   1. ____
   ______________________________ (1 Timothy 1:3–4)
   2. ____
   ______________________________ (Galatians 3:1–3)
   3. ____
   ________________________________ (1 Timothy 1:7)

10. Even today many Christians are willing to believe false teachers. Please give at least four reasons why *you think* this happens.

    1. ____
    ____
    2. ____
    ____
    3. ____
    ____
    4. ____
    ____

11. What *do you think* a Christian can do to protect himself or herself against false teaching?

    ____
    ____
    ____
    ____

Want to learn how to disciple another person, lead a life-changing Bible study or start another study? Go to www.LamplightersUSA.org/training to learn how.

ADDITIONAL INSIGHTS

ADDITIONAL INSIGHTS

Two

Living in Gratitude

Read 1 Timothy 1:8–20; other references as given.

In the first lesson you learned that the church of Jesus Christ and individual believers must stick to the Word of God. Paul commanded Timothy to correct those who were (1) teaching fables as truth, (2) placing unwarranted credence on (Jewish) genealogies, and (3) misinterpreting and misapplying the Old Testament Law of Moses (Mosaic Law, Law, Old Covenant) and making it mandatory for all Christians to obey.

In this second lesson Paul explains the correct use the OT Law (1 Timothy 1:8–11) and then bursts into exuberant praise to God for rescuing him from his sin. As Paul recounts his past sins (blasphemy, persecution, arrogance; 1 Timothy 1:13), he's careful to speak about his past in the past (**I was formerly**). In doing so, he reveals to his readers the key to overcoming a sinful past (1 Timothy 1:12–17). He also warns believers about the consequences of not being grateful to God by identifying two individuals who had suffered spiritual shipwreck in their faith (1 Timothy 1:18–20).

Now ask God to reveal Himself through His Word and conform you into the image of Jesus Christ.

Volunteer Rule:

If the leader asks for volunteers to read, pray, and answer the questions, group members will be more inclined to invite newcomers.

ADD GROUP INSIGHTS BELOW

1. The false teachers' emphasis on the law, fables, and endless genealogies identify them as religious legalizers (Jews or else Gentiles previously converted to Judaism who professed to be believers in Jesus Christ but taught that adherence to the Old Testament Law [Exodus 20:1–Numbers 10:10] was

ADDITIONAL INSIGHTS

mandatory for New Testament Christians; Acts 15:1–5). The Scriptures clearly teach that a Christian is not saved by the Law (Titus 3:5), nor does he mature spiritually by keeping the Law (Galatians 3:1–5). Paul said, however, that **we know that the law is good if one uses it lawfully** (1 Timothy 1:8). What do you think is the correct or lawful use of the OT Law (1 Timothy 1:8–10; Romans 3:20; Galatians 3:19–25)?

2. The phrase **the glorious gospel of the blessed God** (1 Timothy 1:11) refers to the total revelation or embodiment of truth that Paul received from God rather than merely the essential aspects of the salvation message (1 Corinthians 15:1–4). Paul considered it glorious because the gospel had rescued him from the wrath of God and transferred him to the kingdom of God's Son (John 3:36; Colossians 1:13).

   a. In addition to being glorious, how did Paul regard the gospel that had been revealed to him (1 Timothy 1:11; 1 Thessalonians 2:4; Titus 1:3)?

   b. Do you regard the glorious gospel in the same way—as a body of truth that's on loan to you for which you will eventually give an account to God?

3. Many Christians believe Paul was the ultimate example of spiritual maturity. His tireless devotion to God and his dedicated service to others has made him a source of great spiritual encouragement to millions of believers. One of the dominant characteristics of his life was his consistent attitude of thankfulness. List several things for which Paul was grateful (1 Timothy 1:12; Romans 1:8; 1 Corinthians 1:4).

4. Many Christians have experienced a great spiritual struggle over the question of the call to full-time, vocational Christian ministry. Should they "step out in faith," leave their current employment, and prepare for vocational ministry if they are not absolutely certain God has called them? Or should they wait from a "call" from the Lord?

   a. What did Paul do as he attempted to discern God's will for His life regarding full-time Christian service (1 Timothy 1:12)?

   b. What did God do to move Paul into vocational ministry (1 Timothy 1:12)?

59:59 Rule:

Participants appreciate when the leader starts and finishes the studies on time—all in one hour (the 59:59 rule). If the leader doesn't complete the entire lesson, the participants will be less likely to do their weekly lessons and the Bible study discussion will tend to wander.

ADDITIONAL INSIGHTS

ADDITIONAL INSIGHTS

5. Paul's faithful service to God and his consistent attitude of thankfulness were directly related to his assurance that God had forgiven him of his sinful past. The believer's past can either be a ladder to the future or a labyrinth (something extremely complex or tortuous) that cripples his spiritual life, making him a prisoner of his past.

   a. How did Paul assess his life and actions before his salvation (1 Timothy 1:13–15)?

      He proclaimed his ignorance

   b. Why was Paul (and everyone who has been saved) shown mercy even though he had been such an enemy of God?

6. The phrase **exceedingly abundant** (NIV: "poured out on me abundantly") implies a comparison between the grace of God and something else (1 Timothy 1:14). What is God's grace always more abundant than (1 Timothy 1:13; Romans 5:20)?

7. God gave Paul grace and the assurance of His forgiveness so he could overcome the painful memories of a troubled past and live wholeheartedly for the Lord.

a. Take a few minutes to solemnly reflect on your own life. Have you truly appropriated God's grace for salvation (Titus 3:5; Romans 10:9–10, 13; Ephesians 2:8–9)?

b. Have you truly appropriated God's mercy for total forgiveness of your sinful past (2 Corinthians 5:17)? If not, why not bow in prayer right now and ask Him for forgiveness and thank Him for cleansing you?

8. The Bible offers ample evidence of Paul's gratitude (joy, thanksgiving, dedicated service, sacrifice for the sake of the gospel, etc.). What similar evidences do you see in your life that you're truly grateful for God's forgiveness?

9. Many unsaved people think lightly of God's judgment because they continue in a sinful lifestyle without experiencing God's judgment. Why did God patiently endure Paul's sin (and everyone else's sin, including yours) prior to his salvation (1 Timothy 1:16)?

35% Rule:

If the leader talks more than 35% of the time, the group members will be less likely to participate.

ADDITIONAL INSIGHTS

ADDITIONAL INSIGHTS

10. The phrase that by them you may **wage the good warfare** indicates an intense conflict (1 Timothy 1:18). In light of the pastoral requirements listed in this epistle (1 Timothy 3:1–7; especially the prohibition against being **quarrelsome**), the admonition seems contradictory to the general demeanor of a godly pastor. Against whom or what do you think Paul wants Timothy (and all believers, including you) to fight?

11. Paul names two men who had not fought the good fight and had suffered shipwreck regarding their faith.

    a. Why did these two men fail to be faithful to the truth (1 Timothy 1:19; 2 Timothy 2:17–18)?

    Hymenaeus
    Alexander

    b. Why do you think that the use of the word **shipwreck** is such an appropriate word picture to describe someone who falls away from the Lord?

    Brings to mind destruction and inability to move forward

ADDITIONAL INSIGHTS

c. If you are a Christian, what are you doing to prevent yourself from becoming spiritually shipwrecked?

Seeking knowledge

12. What do you think is meant by the statement **whom I delivered to Satan that they may learn not to blaspheme** (1 Timothy 1:20; 1 Corinthians 5:1–8)?

ADDITIONAL INSIGHTS

Gods word stays in your heart

Three

Jesus—Mediator and Ransom

Read 1 Timothy 2:1–7; other references as given.

In the previous lesson Paul explained the proper use the OT Law and praised God for rescuing him from his sin. Paul said he had been a blasphemer, persecutor, and insolent/arrogant prior to being saved (1 Timothy 1:13) . Paul had worked feverishly to destroy the church in its infancy (1 Corinthians 15:9; Galatians 1:13), but God mercifully saved him. How could he not praise God, who had showed him such mercy?

The Bible uses many names to describe Jesus—Christ, Word, Alpha and Omega, Good Shepherd, True Vine, Lamb of God, I AM, the Door, the Truth, the Way, the Life, the Resurrection, the Great High Priest, and many more. In this lesson you will learn two important, but lesser-known, names used to describe Jesus—Mediator and Ransom. You will also learn *how* and *why* we should pray for those whom God has placed as authorities in our lives.

Now ask God to reveal Himself through His Word and conform you into the image of Jesus Christ.

1. The first chapter of 1 Timothy emphasizes the need for correct teaching or theology within the church. The second chapter addresses the need for proper conduct during congregational worship. List three phrases that indicate that the subject of 1 Timothy 2 is corporate worship (1 Timothy 2:8, 11–12).

Focus Rule:

If the leader helps the group members focus on the Bible, they will gain more confidence to study God's Word on their own.

ADD GROUP INSIGHTS BELOW

ADDITIONAL INSIGHTS

2. The phrase **first of all** indicates a major break in thought and highlights the significance of the following passage. The Greek word for **first** (*protos*) means first in time or first in importance. Which meaning of the word *protos* do you think should be used for the correct interpretation in 1 Timothy 2:1?

Importance

3. Throughout church history, the church has struggled to define its relationship to the society in which it finds itself. Should the church (1) attempt to purify society even to the point of establishing a Christian state, (2) isolate itself in an attempt to become a pure church, or (3) live distinctively as witnesses of the truth and representatives for Christ within a sinful world?

   a. Which position/perspective do you think best represents Christ's goal for the church in the world? Why?

   #3

   b. What did the apostle Paul instruct the Philippians believers to do (Philippians 2:14–16)?

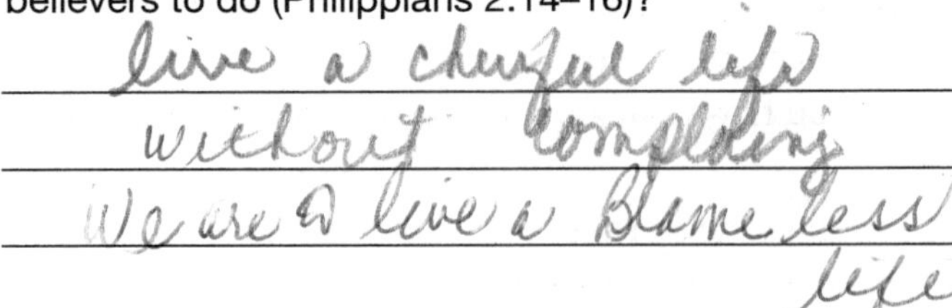

4. It has been said that the church is too worldly and the world is too churchy (meaning it is religious but not necessarily godly).

a. What do you think the church (all born-again believers throughout the world) can do to be better witnesses for Jesus Christ?

b. What one thing could you do to be a better witness for Christ?

5. a. What is the most powerful tool God has given the church to influence society for good (1 Timothy 2:1–2)?

b. Why did Paul specifically urge Timothy (and all Christians by application) to pray for kings and all those in authority (1 Timothy 2:3–4)?

6. a. If prayer is supposed to be a priority for all believers and local churches, do you faithfully pray for those in authority, including unsaved government officials?

Drawing Rule:

Try to draw everyone into the group discussion, but always ask for volunteers.

ADDITIONAL INSIGHTS

ADDITIONAL INSIGHTS

b. What positive changes do you think you could expect in your society if you committed yourself to prayer?

____

____

____

7. Of the seven different Greek words used for prayer in the NT, four are used in 1 Timothy 2:1. The word **prayers** (Gk. *proseuche*, used 37 times in the NT) is the most general word for prayer and it is used for both public and private prayers. The remaining three words for prayer emphasize specific kinds of prayers. List the three other words for prayer and give a brief definition of each (use a dictionary if you wish).

1. ______________________________

____

2. ______________________________

____

3. ______________________________

____

8. Besides praying for the governing officials that God has placed over them, what else does the Bible command all believers to do to influence society for good (Romans 13:1–7)?

____

____

____

9. Some Christians believe the church needs to be more active in social and political reform (protecting the unborn and vulnerable within society, etc.). Others believe the church can become so engrossed in social reform that it can lose

sight of its mission to reach the lost and fulfill the Great Commission (Matthew 28:18–20). What does the Bible teach about the Christian's involvement in social betterment?

1. Matthew 5:13–16: ____________________

2. Mark 14:7: ____________________

3. John 18:36: ____________________

4. Philippians 2:15: ____________________

10. a. The phrase **there is one God and one Mediator between God and men, the Man Christ Jesus** has profound theological implications (1 Timothy 2:5). List at least three.

    1. ____________________

    2. ____________________

    3. ____________________

    b. Since there is only one mediator between God and men, are you absolutely certain that Jesus Christ will be your mediator (Savior) when you stand before God?

    ____

Has your group become a "Holy huddle?" Learn how to reach out to others by taking online leadership training.

ADDITIONAL INSIGHTS

ADDITIONAL INSIGHTS

If you have just realized that Jesus Christ is the *only* mediator before the Father, admit to God that you are a sinner, and call upon Jesus Christ to be your Mediator, Lord and Savior right now (Romans. 10:9, 10, 13).

If you have just trusted Christ for salvation, please tell a spiritual mentor such as your pastor or group leader.

Four

Order in the Church

Read 1 Timothy 2:8–15; other references as given.

In the last lesson you were introduced to two significant words (*mediator*, *ransom*) that describe the person and work of the Lord Jesus. You also learned that believers should pray continually for those in authority so that the gospel may advance throughout the world.

In this lesson you'll learn about God's desire for proper order in worship within the church. Worship expressions of God's church vary greatly throughout the world. A church may meet under a tree in rural Africa and sing traditional African Christian songs and hymns. A church may meet in a darkened room to read the Bible and pray quietly in a closed country. Or a church may meet freely in a nation with religious freedom without fear of persecution. God allows a great degree of freedom in worship expression, but He insists upon certain priorities for all churches. In this lesson, you'll learn what they are and why God has ordained them for all churches in all ages.

Now ask God to reveal Himself through His Word and give you the grace to accept what you will be learning.

Gospel Gold Rule:

Try to get all the answers to the questions—not just the easy ones. Go for the gold.

ADD GROUP INSIGHTS BELOW

1. The use of the definite Greek article *the* in the phrase **that the men** indicates that the men of the church should lead in congregational prayer (1 Timothy 2:8). The phrase **lifting up holy hands, without wrath and doubting** emphasizes the need for moral purity and spiritual consecration during prayer. The Greek word for **holy** (*hosios*) emphasizes

ADDITIONAL INSIGHTS

personal holiness or freedom from sin. Lifting up **holy hands** (1 Kings 8:22; Psalm 141:2; 143:6) indicates an earnest desire on behalf of the individual to come before God in sincerity and truth.

a. Some Christians believe they must be in a specific place or posture when they pray. List three places and postures for prayer mentioned in the Scriptures:

1. Matthew 26:36–39: ______________________

____

2. Luke 18:10–14: ______________________

____

3. Acts 21:5: ______________________

____

b. Paul wanted the men **everywhere to pray** (1 Timothy 2:8). What do you think is meant by this phrase?

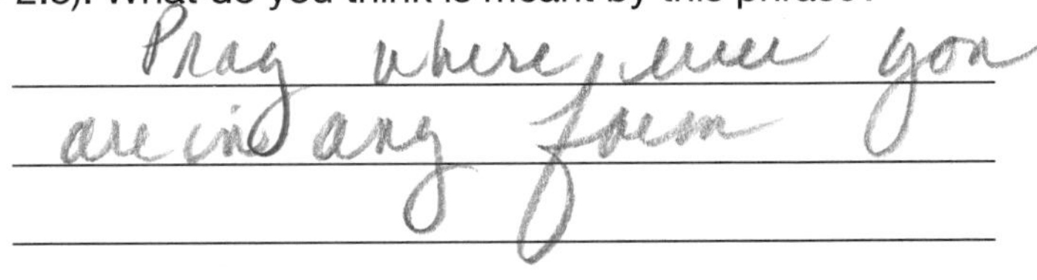

____

2. Christian women are to adorn themselves in **modest apparel** (1 Timothy 2:9). The phrase **in like manner** links this instruction to the preceding discussion, showing that the subject is still public worship services. The Greek word for **modest** (*kosmios*—well-arranged, moderate, modest) could be understood by the modern phrase *in good taste*.

a. The meaning of this biblical command is further explained by the two terms, **propriety and moderation**. What do you think it means for a Christian woman to dress with **propriety and moderation** (1 Timothy 2:9; NIV: "with decency and propriety")?

____

Conservative

b. To what extent (if any) do you think a Christian woman should consider the clothing fashions of a particular society when she determines how to fulfill this biblical command (1 Corinthians 9:20–22)?

With Moderation

3. (Christian women) If another Christian woman asked you how to dress in a manner pleasing to the Lord, what advice would you give her?
(Christian fathers or mothers) If your daughter asked you how she should dress in a manner pleasing to the Lord, what counsel would you give her?

dress conservatively

4. If a Christian woman shouldn't focus on physical beauty, upon what should she place her attention (1 Timothy 2:9–10; 1 Peter 3:3–4)?

Inner Beauty
Relationship w/ God

Balance Rule:

To balance the group discussion, the leader can prepare the lesson by writing the start time in pencil next to each question. To learn how, contact Lamplighters.

ADDITIONAL INSIGHTS

ADDITIONAL INSIGHTS

5. The question of women serving in a spiritual leadership role over men within the local church has often been a matter of intense debate within the church. Those who oppose the concept of women serving in this way often point to 1 Timothy 2:11–12 for scriptural support. Those in favor of women serving in a spiritual leadership capacity offer a variety of arguments to support their position, including Galatians 3:28.

   a. Some dismiss Paul's statement by saying that his statement was motivated by personal prejudice against women. Why should a Christian reject this and all interpretations of the Bible that attribute error in the Scriptures due to the author's prejudice (2 Timothy 3:16–17; 2 Peter 1:20–21)?

      man of God

      who believe

   b. Those who support the inclusion of women in spiritual leadership positions over men within the church point to Galatians 3:25–28. According to this interpretation, salvation in Jesus Christ obliterates (removes any trace of) all racial, social, and gender distinctions. They believe that continuing to promote gender distinction denies the work of the cross. Do you agree with this interpretation of Galatians 3:28 and its application to spiritual leadership within the church? Why?

      Because "God" loves us all equally

6. Some Christians dismiss the apparent prohibition against women teaching or exercising authority over men in the church by saying that the Bible was written in a male-dominated culture that no longer applies in our culture. While it is true that some Bible passages are culturally bound, extreme care should be taken when interpreting the Scriptures so that biblical commands are not ignored.

   a. Do you think the prohibition against women teaching or exercising authority over men (1 Timothy 2:11–12) should be dismissed due to the cultural argument (1 Timothy 2:13–14)? Why?

   all of us are equal in the eyes of God.

   b. Does this prohibition against women teaching or exercising authority over men prevent them from teaching other women and children within the church (Titus 2:3–5)?

   no

   c. Does the Bible prohibit Christian women from offering spiritual instruction to men apart from the corporate worship services of the church (Acts 18:26)?

   no

7. The last verse of the second chapter (1 Timothy 2:15) is perhaps the most difficult verse in 1 Timothy. What do

Did you know Lamplighters is more than a small group ministry? It is a discipleship training ministry that uses a small group format to train disciple-makers. If every group trained one person per study, God would use these new disciple-makers to reach more people for Christ.

ADDITIONAL INSIGHTS

ADDITIONAL INSIGHTS

you think is meant by the phrase **she will be saved in childbearing, if they continue in faith, love, and holiness, with self-control** (1 Timothy 2:15)?

FIVE

DEFINITION OF SPIRITUAL MATURITY

Read 1 Timothy 3:1–7; other references as given.

In 1 Timothy 1 you learned that truth matters. False doctrine leads to worthless disputes that lead to conflict, and believers are not edified. In 1 Timothy 2 you learned that the church can greatly influence the surrounding culture through prayer. You also learned that God has identified certain spiritual priorities for corporate worship.

In this lesson you'll learn the biblical qualifications for leadership within a local church. Gene Getz, author of *The Measure of a Man*, believes these 16 characteristics or qualities can be used to form a profile of a godly man or woman. In this lesson you'll examine several of these spiritual characteristics to see how they might apply to our lives.

Now ask God to reveal Himself through His Word and give you the grace to accept what you will be learning.

No-Trespassing Rule:

To keep the Bible study on track, avoid talking about political parties, church denominations, and Bible translations.

ADD GROUP INSIGHTS BELOW

1. The New Testament uses several terms to describe the office and ministry of church leaders. Although the term **elder** (Gk. *prebuteros*; 1 Peter 5:1) is the most common, other designations such as **bishop** (1 Timothy 3:1), **overseer** (Acts 20:28) and **pastor/teacher** or **shepherd** (Gk. *poimen*; Ephesians 4:11) appear to be used interchangeably in Scripture.

   a. Since all Scripture is inspired by God (2 Timothy 3:16), what do you think is meant by the phrase **This is a**

ADDITIONAL INSIGHTS

faithful saying (1 Timothy 3:1; 4:9)?

b. How does the Bible describe the unique work of pastoral leadership (1 Timothy 3:1)?

2. The spiritual qualifications for leadership within the church have been frequently overlooked. Many congregations and prospective pastoral candidates have glossed over these qualifications and suffered the consequences of their error. What word or phrase indicates that the spiritual qualifications for elders are a prerequisite for pastoral leadership rather than long-range character goals or suggestions?

3. Give at least four reasons why the office of elder or pastor/teacher within a local church is limited to men (1 Timothy 2:11–3:5).

   1.

   2.

   3.

   4.

4. It has been suggested that the 16 spiritual qualifications

for spiritual leadership form an excellent profile of a godly Christian man or woman. Carefully review the qualifications for spiritual leadership (1 Timothy 3:1–7).

a. Look closely at the biblical qualifications for spiritual leadership. Do you think these spiritual qualities would make a good spiritual goal for all believers? Why?

____

____

____

____

____

b. Look closely at the 16 qualifications for spiritual leadership. Circle the ones that could apply to you, and then identify the top three you would most like to see developed more fully in your life.

blameless	husband of one wife
temperate	sober-minded
good behavior	hospitable
able to teach	not given to wine
not violent	not greedy for money
gentle	not quarrelsome
not covetous	one who rules his own house well
having children in submission with reverence	not a novice

____

____

____

If you use table tents or name tags, it will help visitors feel more comfortable and new members will be assimilated more easily into your group.

ADDITIONAL INSIGHTS

ADDITIONAL INSIGHTS

5. Give a brief definition of the following terms:

   1. Temperate: ______________________

   2. Sober-minded (NIV: "self-controlled"): ______________________

   3. Of good behavior (NIV: "respectable"): ______________________

6. a. The elder, pastor/teacher, or bishop **must be blameless** (1Timothy 3:2). What do you think this means?

   b. Why is it unwise for a church to put a novice in a position of spiritual leadership (1 Timothy 3:6)?

   c. What do think is the meaning of the phrase **lest ... he fall into the same condemnation as the devil** (1 Timothy 3:6)?

7. The phrase **husband of one wife** has been variously interpreted (1 Timothy 3:2). Some have understood the phrase to mean that spiritual leaders within a church must be married. Others believe the phrase is a prohibition

against polygamy. Still others say that the pastor cannot be divorced and/or remarried (even in the case of death of a spouse). Another interpretation teaches that the pastor must be fully devoted to the various needs of his wife. Which of the interpretations listed above do you think is the correct interpretation of this difficult phrase?

____

____

____

____

8. Besides the pastor's personal character, the Bible emphasizes the overseer's relationship to his family. Why is it important for a pastor to have a good family (1 Timothy 3:5)?

____

____

____

____

____

9. Pastoral leadership within the church is a demanding responsibility. The weekly preaching and teaching of the Word (including study and prayer), counseling, and outreach, as well as a host of administrative responsibilities, can overwhelm a pastor and his family.

    a. What advice would you offer a young pastor to help him avoid becoming burned out in the pastoral ministry?

    ____

    ____

    ____

    ____

    ____

Use the side margins to write down spiritual insights from other people in your group. Add the person's name and the date to help you remember in the future.

ADDITIONAL INSIGHTS

ADDITIONAL INSIGHTS

b. What do you think you could do to be more of a help and encouragement to the spiritual leaders God has given you?

Six

Servants of God and His Church

Read 1 Timothy 3:8–16; other references as given.

In the last lesson you learned that God calls spiritually qualified Christian servants to oversee His church. The pressure of caring for God's people, faithfully preaching God's Word, refuting theological error, and reaching the lost can be overwhelming at times. Pastoral burnout is not uncommon.

For a church to function well, it also needs faithful servant leaders who assist the elders or pastors and contribute to the effective administration of the ministry. These servants must be biblically qualified and carefully chosen if the church is to function according to God's design. In 1 Timothy 3:8–16 the Bible provides clear instruction about the specific qualifications of deacons and godly women who serve the Lord and His church.

Now ask God to reveal Himself through His Word and give you the grace to accept what you will be learning.

Transformation Rule:

Seek for personal transformation, not mere information, from God's Word.

ADD GROUP INSIGHTS BELOW

1. Having completed the spiritual qualifications for elders or pastor/teachers, Paul now presents the biblical qualifications for the individuals serving as deacons (1 Timothy 3:8–10, 12). What words or phrases indicate that the qualifications for the office of deacon (Gk. *diakonos*—servant) are also prerequisites—not spiritual goals, suggestions, or recommendations (1 Timothy 3:8)?

____

____

ADDITIONAL INSIGHTS

2. The ministry of the deacon/servant is very important to the effective administration of a church. The similarities between the qualifications for deacon and those for pastor/teacher emphasize the high calling of the deacon ministry and the need for the church to choose only biblically qualified individuals.

   a. What similarities do you notice between these two ministries?

   ____

   ____

   ____

   ____

   ____

   b. What important differences do you observe?

   ____

   ____

3. Deacons who serve well are a tremendous help to the work of the Lord. They meet a host of spiritual and practical needs within the church, freeing the pastors so that they can concentrate on the spiritual priorities God has given them (Ephesians 4:12; 1 Timothy 4:13–16; 1 Peter 5:1–3). It is important for the men serving in this ministry to possess certain character qualifications (1 Timothy 3:10).

   a. Deacons are to be **reverent** (1 Timothy 3:8). What do you think this means?

   ____

   ____

   ____

   b. The deacon is not supposed to be **double-tongued** (1 Timothy 3:8). A modern colloquialism or verbal equivalent of this phrase would be *two-faced*. Why do you think it would be important for a deacon not to be double-tongued or two-faced?

____

____

____

____

4. The ministry of the deacon includes assisting the elders or pastors and ministering to the needs of the congregation. For this reason a deacon must not allow himself to be brought into bondage by things that would waste his time and negatively affect his testimony for Christ (1 Timothy 3:8; **not given to much wine**). The deacon should also not be **greedy for money** (1 Timothy 3:8). What do you think are some evidences that a Christian may be characterized by the love of money?

____

____

____

____

5. The list of spiritual qualifications for deacon/servants provides a clear spiritual profile for the ministry so that the church may choose only qualified men. What else did Paul instruct Timothy and the church at Ephesus to do to ensure that only scripturally qualified men serve in this ministry (1 Timothy 3:10)?

____

____

____

____

____

Would you like to learn how to prepare a life-changing Bible study using a simple 4-step process? Contact Lamplighters and ask about ST-A-R-T.

ADDITIONAL INSIGHTS

ADDITIONAL INSIGHTS

6. While the role of the servant is often dishonorable to the world, Jesus Christ said that the one who wishes to be great should be servant of all (Mark 10:43–45). A deacon who serves well will undoubtedly receive an eternal reward for his faithful service. What else does he receive if he serves well (1 Timothy 3:13)?

7. Bible scholars are uncertain about the true identity of the women mentioned in 1 Timothy 3:11. Some interpreters believe the verse refers to the wives of the pastors and deacons while others believe it refers to a third office within the church—the deaconess (the same Greek word for deacon is used of Phoebe in Romans 16:1). A third possibility is that these women are a distinct group who serve in a ministry somewhat similar to the male deacons but hold an unofficial office within the church (note: the spiritual qualifications listed in verse 11 are strikingly similar to those mentioned for the older women in Titus 2:3). Which of the interpretations mentioned above do you think is correct? Why?

8. a. In lesson 1 you considered the original purpose or goal for Paul's letter to Timothy. Restate why the apostle Paul originally wrote this letter to Timothy (1 Timothy 3:14–15).

b. How does Paul describe the church (1 Timothy 3:15)?

____

____

____

9. Paul's statement that the church is the pillar and ground (NIV: "pillar and foundation") of the truth is extremely significant. God has called the church to be more than a conservative copy of a corrupt society, God has called the church to be a beacon of God's Word to a world lost in the sea of sin.

a. In Paul's second letter to Timothy, he told Timothy to **Preach the word! Be ready in season *and* out of season. Convince, rebuke, exhort, with all longsuffering and teaching** (2 Timothy 4:2). Why was Paul so adamant about Timothy preaching the Word (2 Timothy 4:3–4)?

____

____

____

____

b. It has been said the church is often more concerned about winning a popularity contest than winning the praises of a holy God. What do you think the modern church should do to be more of a beacon of (God's) light (pillar and ground of the truth)?

____

____

____

____

10. Paul used the word **mystery** (Gk. *musterion*—something previously hidden but now revealed) when he referred to the confidence a deacon should have in his relationship to

If the leader places a watch on the table, group members will feel confident that the Bible study will be completed on time. If the leader doesn't complete the lesson, group members will be less inclined to do their weekly lessons.

ADDITIONAL INSIGHTS

ADDITIONAL INSIGHTS

God (1 Timothy 3:9). In verse 16 he uses the same word to introduce an early hymn or poem. Who is the one who was manifest in the flesh, **received up in glory,** and becomes the common confession of all believers (1 Timothy 3:6; John 1:14)?

SEVEN

DOCTRINES OF DEMONS

Read 1 Timothy 4:1–5; other references as given.

The message of the first three chapters of 1 Timothy seems simple. The church teaches correct doctrine, believers worship together according to God's prescribed plan, and the church chooses qualified spiritual leaders to oversee the ministry.

But as any godly elder or pastor will tell you, it's not that easy. Satan, working through human agency, preys on the spiritually naive and carnally minded, promoting false doctrine and sowing discord within the church.

Paul's letter to Timothy began with a warning to the young pastor and the church about the dangers of false teaching (1 Timothy 1:3–7). In 1 Timothy 4 Paul returns to his original admonition about being watchful about false teaching and gives specific instruction about how to identify false teachers and the errors they teach as truth.

Now ask God to reveal Himself through His Word and give you the grace to accept what you will be learning.

If the leader asks all the study questions, the group discussion will be more likely to stay on track.

ADD GROUP INSIGHTS BELOW

1. When Paul left Ephesus near the end of his third missionary journey (Acts 18:23–21:16), he solemnly warned the Ephesian elders that false teachers would eventually come into the church (Acts 20:18–35).

   a. How did Paul originally describe these false teachers (Acts 20:29)?

   ____

ADDITIONAL INSIGHTS

b. What did Paul say they would do (Acts 20:28–30)?

______

______

______

2. Paul's prophecy (Acts 20:28–30) was fulfilled when the false teachers came into the Ephesian church (1 Timothy 1:3–7). In 1 Timothy 4, Paul warned Timothy about a specific false teaching—Gnosticism (pronounced *nos-ti-siz-em*, from Gk. *gnosis*—knowledge; 1 Timothy 6:20). Gnosticism began in the late pre-Christian era and gradually developed into a heresy that powerfully affected the church by the late second century AD. Followers of the heresy taught that all matter is inherently evil. Only God, being pure spirit, is good. This naturally led to an emphasis on asceticism, the practice of strict self-denial as a measure of personal religious discipline.

   a. What did Paul say would happen in **latter times** (1 Timothy 4:1)? The phrase **latter times** indicates an unspecified time in the future. The phrase should not be confused with the phrase **the last days** (2 Timothy 3:1; Hebrews 1:2).

   ______

   ______

   b. The word **depart** (Gk. *aphistemi*—to stand away from, apostasize, fall away) indicates a departure of some from a former position of holding firmly to biblical truth. Why did some within the Ephesian church fall away from the truth (1 Timothy 4:1)?

   ______

   ______

3. What do you think is meant by the phrase **deceiving spirits and doctrines of demons** (1 Timothy 4:1)? Do you think the

two phrases are essentially the same? If not, how are they distinct?

____

____

____

____

____

4. Why do you think the Bible refers to this false teaching as the **deceiving spirits and doctrines of demons**?

____

____

____

5. Many Christians are naive when it comes to discerning between true and false religious instruction. Their lack of discernment makes them easy targets for false religious teachers who masquerade as servants of God (2 Corinthians 11:13–15, 20; 2 Peter 2:1–22).

   a. Paul presented two characteristics of the false teachers to help Timothy and others (including us) within the church to identify this dangerous threat. What are they (1 Timothy 4:2–3)?

      1. _______________ (v. ____)

      2. _______________ (v.____)

   b. Religious heresies never die. Satan simply recycles them, and they surface with new names and continue to beguile naive individuals (Hinduism—New Age). Give some modern examples of religious teaching that also forbids marriage and advocates abstaining from certain foods.

      ____

      ____

The Bible says, *So then faith comes by hearing and hearing by the word of God* (Romans 10:17). Every time you humbly study God's Word, your faith grows.

ADDITIONAL INSIGHTS

ADDITIONAL INSIGHTS

6. Many Christians feast on a spiritual smorgasbord of local church preaching, national radio and TV ministries, seminars, conferences, and a variety of other religious teaching. While this much exposure to spiritual instruction should lead to spiritual maturity, it seems that more Christians seem spiritually confused and are ripe for spiritual deception than ever before.

   a. One of the characteristics of false teachers is that their walk (their personal devotion to God) does not match their talk (their religious teaching). Paul called this **speaking lies in hypocrisy** (1 Timothy 4:2). How well do you know the personal spiritual character of the religious teachers (pastors, Christian leaders) who influence your spiritual thinking?

   b. If you found out that one of your favorite spiritual mentors (pastor, speaker) was ethically or morally corrupt, do you think you should continue to follow the spiritual leaders' teaching even if you felt as if you were benefiting from their ministry? Why?

7. Gnosticism attempted to change Christianity into a philosophy of life. The Gnostics believed that knowledge (Gk. *gnosis*) was superior to faith, and only certain individuals possessed this special enlightenment. The Gnostic leaders used their self-proclaimed "enlightenment" to control their followers. This form of spiritual entrapment has resurfaced many times throughout church history.

   a. The false religious teachers told their followers not to marry and to abstain from eating certain foods (1 Timothy 4:3). What does the Bible say about marriage and the food God has created (Hebrews 13:4; 1 Timothy 4:3–4)?

   ____

   ____

   ____

   ____

   ____

   b. Paul said that nothing is to be rejected **if it is received with thanksgiving; for it is sanctified by the word of God and prayer** (1 Timothy 4:4–5). What do you think this means?

   ____

   ____

   ____

   ____

   ____

8. The thought that God allows false teachers within the church is bewildering to many believers. Why does a loving, righteous God allow spiritual charlatans to draw people away from the truth (Deuteronomy 13:1–3)?

   ____

It's a good time to begin praying and inviting new people for your next Open House.

ADDITIONAL INSIGHTS

ADDITIONAL INSIGHTS

Eight

Walk the Talk

Read 1 Timothy 4:6–16; other references as given.

In the previous lesson Paul gave Timothy specific instruction about the character and conduct of false teachers. Paul identified the source of their error (doctrines of demons), addressed their ungodly character (liars, hypocrites with seared consciences), and even identified the false doctrines they peddled as truth.

But could Timothy do anything to counteract their error beside commanding them to not teach their heresies? Absolutely. Paul told Timothy to teach the truth (1 Timothy 4:6), reject error (1 Timothy 4:7), and live a godly life (1 Timothy 4:8–16)—the same things every true follower of Jesus Christ can do to honor God and counteract error. In this lesson you'll see how important it is for the walk of Christians to match their talk.

Now ask God to reveal Himself through His Word and to give you grace to accept what you will be learning.

Is your study going well? Consider starting a new group. To learn how, go to www.LamplightersUSA.org/training.

ADD GROUP INSIGHTS BELOW

1. Paul instructed Timothy to confront the religious legalists because their teaching was causing spiritual confusion in the church (1 Timothy 1:3–4).

   a. What three things was Timothy to do to protect himself and the church against this second attack of false teaching (1 Timothy 4:6–7)?

      1. Be a good menister of Jesus Christ (v. ____)

ADDITIONAL INSIGHTS

2. ______________________________
______________________________ (v. ____)
3. ______________________________
______________________________ (v. ____)

b. Timothy would be a **good minister** (Gk. *diakonos*—deacon, servant, minister) of Christ Jesus if he faithfully taught the truth and warned the church about false teaching (1 Timothy 4:6). Do you think the same designation applies to all believers (clergy and lay believers) if they faithfully and lovingly stand for the truth and warn other believers about the threat of spiritual deception? Why?

____

____

____

2. Paul warned Timothy and the Ephesian church about religious teachers who promoted man-made systems of spiritual worship. Paul also rebuked some of the Thessalonian believers who were living undisciplined lives (2 Thessalonians 3:7–11).

a. If believers are not supposed to adopt man-made religious restrictions, but they are to live disciplined lives (1 Corinthians 9:19–27), what must they do to accomplish this spiritual objective (1 Timothy 4:7)?

____

____

____

____

b. The phrase **exercise yourself toward godliness** (1 Timothy 4: 7–8; Gk. *gumnasia*—exercise, train, gymnasium) expresses the idea of self-denial and a determined effort to reach a desired goal. If every Christian's goal is true godliness, what specific things are you doing to reach the goal of spiritual godliness?

3. What do you think is the difference between being godly and merely being religious?

4. Paul worked hard to reach his goal of godliness. The words **labor** (Gk. *kopiao*—to grow weary) and **suffer** (1 Timothy 4:10; Gk. *agonizomai*—to agonize) are strong terms that describe the intensity of Paul's efforts to live for God and his willingness to endure hardship. Why was Paul willing to labor so diligently for God (1 Timothy 4:8)?

5. The phrase **the Savior of all men, especially of those who believe** has been the cause of much debate (1 Timothy 4:10). There are four main interpretations:
(1) *The Universalist View*. God will eventually save all men.
(2) *The Providential View*. God saves (preserves; Acts 17:25) all men by giving them life and sustenance.
(3) *The Potential-actual View*. God is the Savior of all men, but only those who trust in Christ will actually be saved (1 Timothy 4:10).

It's time to choose your next study. Turn to the back of the study guide for a list of available studies or go online for the latest studies.

ADDITIONAL INSIGHTS

ADDITIONAL INSIGHTS

(4) *The Temporal-eternal View*. God is the Savior of all men giving them temporal life and sustenance, but He especially gives life (eternal) to those who are called and believe (trust) in Christ for eternal life. Which interpretation do you think is correct? Why?

____

____

____

____

____

6. Many young Christians are tempted to believe that they can't have a significant ministry for God until they are older. Timothy, however, was a young pastor who was greatly used of God.

   a. What three things was Timothy to do as a young pastor to help the church accept Paul's instructions (1 Timothy 4:11–12)?

      1. ______________________________________

         ____

      2. ______________________________________

         ____

      3. ______________________________________

         ____

   b. Name the six specific areas of godly conduct in which Timothy (and all Christians by application) was to be an example (1 Timothy 6:11).

      1. ________________________________ (v. ____)

      2. ________________________________ (v. ____)

      3. ________________________________ (v. ____)

4. ________________________________ (v. ____)
5. ________________________________ (v. ____)
6. ________________________________ (v. ____)

7. It has been said that the church is a mile wide and an inch deep. Part of the reason for the shallowness of many believers' faith is the lack of sound Bible teaching in the churches and many religious teachers appear to be unaware of the biblical pattern of communicating God's Word.

   a. What was Timothy to do to help the Ephesian believers become spiritually mature (1 Timothy 4:13)?

   ____

   ____

   ____

   b. In Paul's second letter to Timothy, he also encouraged Timothy to preach the Word (2 Timothy 4:2). In his first letter to the Corinthians, Paul reminded them that he did not use persuasive words of human wisdom when he originally preached to them (1 Corinthians 2:1–5). Why did Paul emphasize the Word of God (the testimony of God; 2 Timothy 1:8) so much in his preaching and teaching (1 Corinthians 2:1–5)?

   ____

   ____

   ____

8. Every believer receives a spiritual gift to be used for the edification of the body of Christ (1 Corinthians 12:7, 11). While some Christians overemphasize the importance of spiritual gifts, other believers almost ignore them entirely. Why did Paul instruct Timothy to not neglect the spiritual gift he was given (1 Timothy 4:14–15)?

____

You can be trained to fulfill the Great Commission. You can take the first step by taking Level 1 (Basic Training), using the student workbook in the back of this study guide. You can take the training individually or as a group.

ADDITIONAL INSIGHTS

ADDITIONAL INSIGHTS

9. Timothy was to pay close attention to his personal walk with the Lord and to his public communication of the Word (1 Timothy 4:16). What do you think is meant by the statement **you will save both yourself and those who hear you**?

Nine

Care and Correction

Read 1 Timothy 5; other references as given.

Paul has addressed the church's need for doctrinal purity and the necessity for maintaining a biblical perspective regarding corporate worship and spiritual leadership (1 Timothy 1–4). He exhorted Timothy to confront false teaching (chapter 1), promote correct worship (chapter 2), select qualified leaders (chapter 3), and conduct himself in a godly manner (chapter 4).

Beginning in 1 Timothy 5, Paul gives Timothy specific instructions about how to minister to and care for various individuals and groups within the church, including those in need (widows). He also instructs Timothy and the church how to relate to the spiritual leaders God has placed over them.

Now ask God to reveal Himself through His Word and give you the grace to accept what you will be learning.

Many groups study the Final Exam the week after the final lesson for three reasons: (1) someone might come to Christ, (2) believers gain assurance of salvation, (3) group members learn how to share the gospel.

ADD GROUP INSIGHTS BELOW

1. a. Listed below are the first four individuals and groups to whom Timothy was to minister. Briefly describe how he was to respond or relate to each of them (Timothy 5:1–2).

   1. Older men: ______________________________

   2. Younger men: ______________________________

   3. Older women: ______________________________

   4. Younger women: ______________________________

ADDITIONAL INSIGHTS

b. Take a minute to evaluate how you relate to others. Do you speak to individuals within the various groups listed above according to the biblical pattern, or do you usually speak whatever is on your mind without considering your audience or manner of speaking?

What could you change to reflect Christ more in your relations with other people?

___

___

___

2. Timothy was to speak with God's authority when he spoke publicly and privately (1 Timothy 4:11). A pastor should not see preaching the Word as an option to be considered but as a divine imperative to be obeyed (2 Timothy 4:2–4). The most common Greek word for preach (*kerusso*—preach, herald, proclaim) was used to describe a herald who delivered the king's message to the people. Similarly, the NT pastor is a herald or messenger who delivers decrees from the King of kings—Jesus Christ. What difference(s) do you notice between the pastor's public preaching and his private ministry to individual believers (1 Timothy 5:1–2; 2 Timothy 2:24–26)?

___

___

___

___

3. The elder or pastor is supposed to minister to the **younger women as sisters, with all purity** (1 Timothy 5:2). Besides the obvious prohibition against immoral impropriety, what else do you think would be included in the meaning of this phrase?

___

___

4. The early church took its responsibility for meeting the needs of the poor, especially widows, very seriously (Acts. 6:1). From the second to fourth century, the church had a Widow Office within the church, whose primary function was to engage in prayer and acts of mercy. Paul instructed Timothy and the Ephesian church to honor widows who are really or truly widows (1 Timothy 5:3). Study the following verses carefully to determine the specific meaning of the word **honor** (1 Timothy 5:3–11, 16). Now explain in your own words what you think is meant by the statement **honor widows who are really widows** (1 Timothy 5:3).

____

____

____

____

____

5. Although the Scriptures teach that the church should do everything possible to meet the physical needs of believers who are in need (James 2:15–16), the church must not simply become a welfare organization.

   a. To whom should a Christian widow (and others in need, by application) turn *before* she looks to the church for financial help (1 Timothy 5:4, 8, 16)?

   ____

   b. What does the Bible say about a believer who is unwilling (not unable) to meet the financial needs of his family (1 Timothy 5:8)?

   ____

   ____

   c. Why would a Christian man be considered **worse than an unbeliever** if he's not willing to meet the financial

Having trouble with your group? A Lamplighters trainer can help you solve the problem.

ADDITIONAL INSIGHTS

ADDITIONAL INSIGHTS

needs of his family (Matthew 5:43–47; James 4:17)?

6. The Bible presents ten qualifications that widows must meet before they can receive regular financial assistance from the church (1 Timothy 5:5, 9–10). What differences do you notice between God's plan for the church to care for the needy and many modern government welfare programs?

7. Instead of looking to the church for financial assistance, younger widows are encouraged to remarry (1 Timothy 5:11, 14). What do you think is meant by the phrase **they have cast off their first faith** (1 Timothy 5:12)?

8. Pastors who work hard at preaching and teaching are **worthy of double honor** (1 Timothy 5:17). Many Bible scholars are uncertain about the exact meaning of this statement. Should the pastors receive twice as much financial assistance as the qualified widows, or should they receive twice the normal rate of pastoral support? Another possible interpretation says elders are worthy of double

honor (worth twice the compensation of those who don't work hard at preaching and teaching). What do you think this phrase means (1 Timothy 5:17–18)?

It's time to order your next study. Allow enough time to get the books so you can distribute them at the Open House. Consider ordering 2-3 extra books for newcomers.

ADDITIONAL INSIGHTS

9. Church leaders can easily become targets of criticism and accusation. Paul instructed Timothy to not accept accusations against fellow elders unless there were two or three sworn witnesses (1 Timothy 5:19–20).

   a. Do you think the phrase **those who are sinning** refers to the sinning pastors or the false witnesses who continue to bring unfounded accusations against spiritual leaders (1 Timothy 5:20)? Why?

   b. Timothy was to rebuke those who continued to sin **before all** (1 Timothy 5:20). If the ones who were sinning refer to the elders or pastors, do you think Timothy was to rebuke them in the presence of all the other pastors or the entire church assembly? Why?

ADDITIONAL INSIGHTS

10. Some churches fail to obey God's plan for restoring a sinning believer to fellowship with the local assembly because they believe it is unloving to confront another believer with his or her sin. Unfortunately, their failure enables the erring believer to continue in a destructive sin pattern and eventually destroy the entire church (1 Corinthians 5:1–6).

    a. If Timothy was obedient to Paul's instruction regarding this difficult aspect of ministry, what positive effect would result from his actions (1 Timothy 5:20)? Please answer in your own words.

    ____

    ____

    ____

    ____

    b. At first glance the exact meaning of 1 Timothy 5:24–25 is difficult to determine. These two verses, however, teach an important truth about the selection of qualified (church) leaders. What is it?

    ____

    ____

    ____

    ____

TEN

THE GOOD FIGHT OF FAITH

Read 1 Timothy 6; other references as given.

Paul wrote pointedly about how Christians should conduct themselves within the church of Jesus Christ. In 1 Timothy 6, Paul (1) instructs slaves—by application, employees—how to relate to both unsaved and saved masters/employers (1 Timothy 6:2), (2) warns Timothy again about false teachers (1 Timothy 6:3–5) and the love of money (1 Timothy 6:6–10), and (3) exhorts him to fight the good fight of faith (1 Timothy 6:11–16, 20–21). He concludes the letter with a challenge to wealthy Christians, encouraging them to set their affection on eternal riches (1 Timothy 6:17–19).

Now ask God to reveal Himself through His Word and give you the grace to accept what you will be learning.

Final Exam:

Are you meeting next week to study the Final Exam? To learn how to present it effectively, contact Lamplighters.

ADD GROUP INSIGHTS BELOW

1. a. Some Christians forfeit a tremendous opportunity to be good witnesses for Christ by not doing a good job at work. What did Paul say would be the result if the Ephesian believers failed to honor their masters in the workplace (1 Timothy 6:1)?

   ____

   ____

   b. Can you honestly say that your work ethic, your quality of work, and your attitude demonstrate respect for your

ADDITIONAL INSIGHTS

employer and are a good witness for Christ? Perhaps you could write down some specific changes that would help you be a more effective witness for Christ.

____

____

____

____

____

2. a. Paul warns Timothy and the Ephesian believers about the threat of false teachers (1 Timothy 6:3–5). Name the two previous groups of false teachers and briefly describe the error of their teaching.

   1. 1 Timothy 1:3–7: _______________

   ____

   ____

   2. 1 Timothy 4:1–4: _______________

   ____

   ____

   b. How does the Bible further describe the enemies of the truth in 1 Timothy 6:4–5?

   ____

   ____

   ____

3. It is difficult to determine whether Paul's third warning about false teachers is referring to another group of false religious teachers or whether he is adding characteristics of those previously mentioned. These false teachers had been **destitute of the truth** (1 Timothy 6:5). The Greek word (*apostereo*) conveys the idea that these men were being robbed of something to which they had a right. Besides

being proud (1 Timothy 6:4), why were these men not able to maintain a biblical perspective (1 Timothy 6:5)?

____

____

____

4. Although many false teachers use religion as a means of financial gain, **godliness with contentment is great gain** (1 Timothy 6:6). What do you think this means?

____

____

____

____

____

5. Give four reasons why Christians should not allow themselves to become mentally and physically consumed with building their own earthly empire (1Timothy 6:7; Ecclesiastes 2:11–23; 2 Timothy 2:4).

   1. ____________________________________

      ____________________________ (________)

   2. ____________________________________

      ____________________________ (________)

   3. ____________________________________

      ____________________________ (________)

   4. ____________________________________

      ____________________________ (________)

6. If the Bible teaches Christians to be content with the basic provisions of life (1 Timothy 6:8, food and clothing), do you think it's wrong for a believer to aggressively pursue a business or professional career or engage in a potentially

Leadership Training:

Do you know that all your Bible study participants can learn to lead life-changing Bible studies? Simply schedule a Level 1 (Basic Training) event for the week after the Final Exam. Your student workbook is in the back of your study guide. Contact Lamplighters to register or for more information.

ADDITIONAL INSIGHTS

ADDITIONAL INSIGHTS

profitable business venture? Why?

7. a. The first part of 1 Timothy 6:10 is one of the most misquoted verses in the Bible. If money is not the root of all kinds of evil, what is the source of all sorts of evil (1 Timothy 6:9–10)?

   b. List six negative results of *desiring* to get rich (1 Timothy 6:9–10):

      1. __________
      2. __________
      3. __________
      4. __________
      5. __________
      6. __________

8. As a young pastor Timothy was to flee from the temptation to be motivated by financial gain or to be not content with God's provision (1 Timothy 6:11, **these things**). The Greek word for **flee** (*pheuge*) is a present imperative verb, which means Paul was commanding Timothy to be constantly fleeing these things.

   a. What do you think the particular verbal form of the word **flee** teaches about Satan's method of attack on believers and their need to escape temptation?

b. Paul told Timothy to keep fleeing from these things (1 Timothy 6:11). What else was Timothy to do to escape from these temptations (1 Timothy 6:11–14)?

c. Are you diligent to do these things so that you can avoid Satan's trap (1 Timothy 6:9–10), or do you find yourself sometimes wandering away from the faith?

Note: If a desire to get rich is causing you to be inconsistent in your devotion to God (wandering away from the faith) and you haven't been able to gain victory in this area of your spiritual life, what do you think you should do to gain the victory God wants you to have?

9. In Paul's charge (Gk. *paraggello*—charge, command, order) to Timothy he mentions several attributes or characteristics of God the Father (1 Timothy 6:13–16). Please name four:

1. ______________________________ (v. ____)

2. ______________________________ (v. ____)

3. ______________________________ (v. ____)

For more discipleship help, sign up to receive the Disciple-Maker Tips—a bi-monthly email that provides insights to help your small group function more effectively.

ADDITIONAL INSIGHTS

ADDITIONAL INSIGHTS

4. ______________________________
______________________________ (v. ____)

10. Christians cannot avoid being exposed to many of the temptations in this world. However, certain believers face special temptations that are unique to their position in life. For example, those who are especially gifted may be tempted to be proud, and the poor may be tempted to doubt God's provision.

    a. What are the two special temptations of the rich (1 Timothy 6:17)?

        1. ______________________________
        ____

        2. ______________________________
        ____

    b. What are the top two temptations you fight and what is your plan to be victorious?

        1. ______________________________
        ____

        2. ______________________________
        ____

11. For the last time in the letter Paul exhorts Timothy to guard (Gk. *phylaxon*—keep, maintain, guard) the deposit or trust of truth given to him (1Timothy 6:20). What was Timothy to do as pastor to protect the church from any further spiritual defection (1 Timothy 6:20)?

____
____
____
____

ADDITIONAL INSIGHTS

12. List the main spiritual truths that were taught in this study. Be willing to share your insights as an encouragement to other members of your discussion group.

ADDITIONAL INSIGHTS

LEADER'S GUIDE

Lesson 1: Stick to the Word

1. God instructed Paul to write 1 Timothy to instruct Timothy (and all believers throughout the ages) and the church at Ephesus how to conduct themselves within an assembly. Paul also told Timothy that the church was to be the pillar and foundation of the truth.

2. Timothy demonstrated childlike obedience to the apostle Paul. Timothy was loyal and devoted to Paul and served him the way a loving son would serve his father.

3. a. God our Father and the Lord Jesus Christ.
   b. Answers will vary.

4. 1. Paul told Timothy to instruct certain religious teachers in the Ephesian church to stop teaching false doctrines.
   2. Timothy and other believers in the church weren't to listen to the fables or endless genealogies.

5. 1. These false teachings would only produce disputes and conflicts (1 Timothy 1:4).
   2. The church would not experience spiritual growth (1 Timothy 1:4, **rather than godly edification**).

6. a. The goal of all Bible instruction is godly behavior that is motivated and characterized by Christlike love. Paul's goal in his preaching and teaching was to see lives changed into the image of Christ—the embodiment of love (1 John 4:8). This should be the goal of all spiritual instruction. Those who are given the opportunity to teach the Word of God should teach to transform rather than to simply inform (Hebrews 4:1–2).
   b. 1. A pure heart.
      2. A good conscience.
      3. A sincere faith.

7. "from which some"

8. 1. The false teachers focused their spiritual teaching on theological speculations (fables) and placed an inordinate emphasis on human tradition (endless genealogies) rather than God's Word (1 Timothy 1:4).
   2. They were not careful to maintain a close personal walk with the Lord. As a result, they allowed sin to exist in their lives and their consciences became defiled which resulted in a shallow and insincere faith (1 Timothy 1:5).
   3. The focus of their spiritual instruction was fruitless discussion, and they did not understand the relationship of the OT Law to the NT believer (1 Timothy 1:6–7). Consequently, they were theologically confused on the subject of law and grace.

9. 1. They promoted themselves and professed to be religious teachers even though they did not know God's Word (1 Timothy 1:3; 1 Timothy 1:4).
   2. The false teachers' emphasis on the religious regulations of the OT Law would have been perceived as spiritual zeal and dedication rather than what it was—error (1 Timothy 1:4; Galatians 3:1–3).
   3. The false teachers spoke boldly, which gave the impression that they possessed strong biblical convictions (1 Timothy 1:7).

10. 1. Many believers are not willing to personally study the Scriptures to determine what the Bible really teaches. They become easy targets for false religious teachers.
    2. Many Christians only want to hear positive things about God and themselves (2 Timothy 4:2–4). As a result, they turn away from the rich teaching of the Word to nonbiblical topics.
    3. Many Christians are confused about God's means of communicating His word in this age. Some false teachers promote the idea that they have received special revelation from God (visions, new insights, dreams, etc.; Hebrews 1:1–2; Jude 3).
    4. Some false teachers have focused their entire teaching ministries on practical applications without teaching the foundational doctrinal beliefs ("The six easy steps to successful Christian living" or "The five easy steps to financial freedom," etc.). This has produced a shallow

church that does not see the need for a solid theological foundation on which to evaluate the practical teachings they receive.

5. Many false teachers have charismatic personalities and are winsome communicators. Other answers could apply.

11. A Christian should study God's Word daily, be an active part of a Bible-believing church, pray that God would not lead him or her into temptation, and serve the Lord faithfully. Answers will vary.

Lesson 2: Living in Gratitude

1. The OT Law is a tutor or schoolmaster that helps people understand their need for salvation in Christ (Galatians 3:24; 1 Timothy 1:9–10). The Greek word for tutor (*paidagogos*) was used of a trusted household slave who was given the entire responsibility of teaching the young Greek and Roman children moral instruction until the time they were handed over to their fathers who would legally adopt their children and recognize them as adults. The child never returned to the care of the tutor. In the same way the Law is man's tutor that instructs him regarding the moral standards of the father (in this case, God) and shows him his need for the Savior. When a man comes to Christ, he is handed over to God the Father, who legally adopts him into His family (Galatians 4:5–7). The new believer is under grace (Romans 6:14) and should never return to the authority of the Law as a motivation for Christian living. To do so, Paul says, would be foolishness (Galatians 3:1–3). Note: This does not mean that the believer is without moral or ethical restraint or direction. The Christian will be judged by the law of Christ or the perfect law of liberty (Galatians 6:2; James 2:12).

2. a. Paul regarded it as a sacred trust. A trust is a property interest held by one person for the benefit of another. In this case, it is God who benevolently gives Christians a body of revelation (the gospel) and they are to manage this trust in accordance with the stated provisions of the trust agreement (the word of God).
   b. Answers will vary.

3. 1. He was thankful for the opportunity to serve the Lord Jesus (1 Timothy 1:12).
   2. He was thankful for other Christians, including those he had never met

(Romans1:8).

3. He was thankful for the spiritual successes of other believers (Romans 1:8).
4. He was thankful for the grace that God had given to other Christians even though they were not manifesting Christlike love toward one another (1 Corinthians 1:4).

4. a. He was faithful to the spiritual responsibilities God had given him. Instead of worrying about where and how God wanted to use him in the future, Paul concentrated on fulfilling the ministries that God had entrusted to him.
   b. God put him into ministry or appointed him to His service (1 Timothy 1:12). This means that God directly intervened in Paul's life in such a way that it was obvious what he was to do.

5. a. As exceedingly sinful. He said he was formerly a blasphemer, a persecutor, and an insolent/arrogant man (1 Timothy 1:13). He also said he was the chief of all sinners. Perhaps he said this because he fought directly against the work of God by persecuting the church. It is important to note that while Paul was quick to admit his sin, he did not glory in it. He didn't gloss over the past, glorify the past, rationalize his sinful behavior, or deny its existence.
   b. Before he was saved, he acted ignorantly in unbelief (1 Timothy 1:13).

6. God's grace is always more abundant than man's sin. There has never been a person who sinned so greatly that God's grace was not able to save him or her.

7. a. Answers will vary.
   b. Answers will vary.

8. Answers will vary, but could include the following: An increase in joy and an attitude of gratitude, a willingness to serve others for the pure joy of helping them and serving Jesus Christ, a willingness to forfeit the pursuit of worldly endeavors so that Christ might be glorified.

9. God patiently endured Paul's sinful life so that Jesus Christ's perfect patience might be revealed. Paul's life was a powerful demonstration of

divine grace.

10. Timothy was to fight the fight of faith by staying true to the Lord and combating error. He was to do this, fulfilling his scriptural responsibility as a pastor, by making sure that theological error did not creep into the church. Timothy was also to keep his own heart free from sin (**having faith**; 1 Timothy 1:19) and maintain a good conscience that comes from having a personal walk with the Lord and doing all that he could to maintain good relationships with others (1 Timothy 1:19).

11. a. Hymenaeus and Alexander did not fight the good fight of faith and as a result allowed sin to control their lives, which caused their consciences to become defiled. Hymenaeus is mentioned as a heretical teacher in 2 Timothy 2:17. There are two Alexanders mentioned in connection with the church at Ephesus. Alexander the coppersmith did Paul great harm (2 Timothy 4:14). Perhaps he is the one mentioned here.
    b. 1. A captain of a ship does not often see the hidden danger of rocks, reefs, and other obstructions that could destroy the ship. In the same way, a lax believer does not always see the spiritual dangers that lie ahead.
       2. A shipwreck caused great and in some cases total destruction to the ship. In the same way, believers who have suffered spiritual shipwreck often experience lifelong consequences as a result of their spiritual lethargy. Other answers could apply.
    c. Answers will vary.

12. It is difficult to determine the exact meaning of this phrase. The other use of this phrase (1 Corinthians 5:5) seems to indicate excommunication from the church, which results in the individual being turned over to Satan's domain (2 Corinthians 4:4).

Lesson 3: Jesus—Mediator and Ransom

1. 1. **I desire therefore that men pray everywhere** (1 Timothy 2:8).
   2. **Let** [the women] **learn in silence** (1 Timothy 2:11).
   3. **I do not permit a woman to teach or to have authority over a man** (1 Timothy 2:12). Note: The generous use of the plural (men, women, 1Timothy 2:8–10, 15) supports the idea that a corporate setting is in

view.

2. It probably means first in importance. Although no specific references may be offered as proof, the emphasis in the chapter (especially through verse eight) is on the importance of prayer.

3. a. #3. The church is called to live godly amidst a sinful world.
   b. Believers are to do everything without grumbling or arguing so they be recognized by the world as God's children. They are to be blameless, sincere and wholesome, living in a sinful world as lights shining in a dark place.

4. a. Pray, live holy lives, resist the world's values and priorities, forsake sin, and live in peace and harmony with others. Other answers could apply.
   b. Answers will vary.

5. a. Specific, believing prayer.
   b. Paul wanted Timothy to teach the Ephesian church to pray for these individuals so that they might live a quiet and peaceable life. God's provision of a quiet and peaceable life for the Christian community was not merely for their personal comfort but so that a conducive social atmosphere might exist for effective evangelism (1 Timothy 2:4).

6. a. Answers will vary.
   b. Answers will vary.

7. 1. Supplications (Gk. *deeseis*) comes from the Greek verb *deomai*—to need. It considers prayer as an expression of need. When a believer entreats God to meet his needs, he is expressing humility (by admitting his inability to provide for himself) and faith (by asking God to meet his needs and bless his life).
   2. Intercessions (Gk. *enteuxeis*). The verbal form of this word means to "fall in with a person, to draw near so as to converse familiarly." It means to draw near to God in confident, childlike faith (Hebrews 4:14–16).
   3. Giving of thanks (Gk. *eucharistias*) is the giving of thanks for the person of God, the plan of God and the provision of God. It reveals an attitude

of confidence in His sovereignty, His moral goodness, and His unfailing love for His people.

8. God commands believers to be subject to all governing authorities, knowing that they are ordained by God (Romans 13:1–7). This includes paying all taxes and obeying the law.

9. 1. The Bible teaches that Christians are to be salt and light. This means that God's people cannot isolate themselves from society to the point that they cease to be a witness for Christ (Matthew 5:13–16).
   2. The church must realize that its primary purpose within God's program is not social reform. Christ said that you will have the poor with you always (Mark 14:7).
   3. Christians should not neglect the many opportunities within society to help, but they must realize that Christ did not come to build an earthly kingdom (John 18:36).
   4. Many of the social problems within a society are a result of the spiritual needs of a particular culture. Striving to solve the world's problems by social reform is often an attempt to relieve the symptom and ignore the cause. God's people should live godly lives and do all they can to help (Philippians 2:15).

10. a. 1. Man in his natural state is estranged from God. The necessity of a mediator indicates that hostility exists between God and man.
       2. Man cannot be his own mediator. A mediator is a third party who seeks and decrees a reconciliation between two or more parties.
       3. There is only one mediator who is able to reconcile the division between God and man. No other mediator is qualified to serve in this capacity (John 14:6).
       4. Jesus Christ is the only mediator between God the Father and man.
       5. Jesus Christ had to exist in human form to become the acceptable mediator (the man Christ Jesus). Certain other answers could apply.
    b. Answers will vary.

Lesson 4: Order in the Church

1. a. 1. Jesus fell on His face in an olive orchard and prayed (Matthew 26:36–39).
   2. The Pharisee and the tax-gatherer stood and prayed at the temple in Jerusalem (Luke 18:10–14).
   3. Paul and others knelt and prayed on a beach (Acts 21:5).

   b. In every church. The early church came together in various places to worship God. The church was an assembly of believers who were organized according to the New Testament pattern.

2. a. Propriety (Gk. *aidos*—modesty) signifies a discretion that shrinks from overstepping the limits of womanly reserve. The godly Christian woman who accepts the biblical standard of modesty will reject that portion of the fashion industry's promotion of apparel that does not glorify the Lord.
   Moderation (Gk. *sophrosyne*) means self-control or self-restraint and identifies the need for self-mastery in the area of passions and desires. When it is used in this context (proper dress) it means the self-discipline to resist all temptations to become obsessed by the latest clothing fashions and the spiritual wisdom to dress practically and sensibly. The Greek word *sophronas* may be translated "sensible" (Titus 1:8; 2:2, 5, 6).

   b. The apostle Paul was sensitive to the culture and the people to which he ministered (1 Corinthians 9:19–20). He adjusted to the culture on nonbiblical issues so that he might identify with them and win them to Christ. A Christian woman should attempt to dress fashionably as long as she does not become obsessed with the latest fashions and violate God's standard of modesty. Other answers could apply.

3. (Both) She should dress in such a way that her appearance does not unnecessarily give any hint of sexual enticement. She should dress "in good taste" in order to be a worthy representative of Christ and be a good witness to the people around her.

4. She should focus on doing good works (1 Timothy 2:10) and allowing God to develop a meek and quiet spirit within her (1 Peter 3:4).

5. a. This interpretation denies the doctrine of inerrancy. It was not Paul's

thoughts or "prejudices" that are written; it's the Word of God (2 Timothy 3:16–17; 2 Peter 1:20–21).

b. Paul's teaching in Galatians 3 does not contradict his teaching in 1 Timothy 2. Galatians 3 deals with the equal access of all people to God through faith in Christ. There are not gradations or various degrees of salvation. All who come to Christ in faith are saved regardless of their ethnic, social, or gender distinctiveness (Galatians 3:26). First Timothy 2, however, deals with how believers function within the church of God. While all who have been saved are equally accepted into the body of Christ, there are certain restrictions for those serving as spiritual leaders within the church.

6. a. Paul's argument against the inclusion of women in a position of teaching or leading men in the church is supported by a transcultural argument—the creative order of man (1 Timothy 2:13–14). Paul's argument reaches far outside the NT culture, indicating that what is being taught is not a cultural peculiarity, but a cross-cultural biblical priority.

b. No. In another pastoral epistle Paul endorsed the older women teaching the younger women (Titus 2:3–5). There is nothing in Scripture that prohibits godly Christian women from ministering (including teaching) in the local church except when it involves teaching men or exercising administrative authority over them.

c. No. Both Aquila and Priscilla taught Apollos the way of the Lord more accurately (Acts 18:26).

7. The four basic views regarding the correct interpretation of this verse are summarized as follows:

1. Women will be physically saved (delivered from death) if they continue in faith and love and sanctity with self-restraint. The glaring weakness of this view is that it is not always true because some godly women have died giving birth.
2. Women shall be spiritually saved through childbearing. This interpretation must also be rejected because it teaches "works salvation" and denies the work of Christ.
3. Women will be saved through childbirth (the birth of Jesus Christ). This is an indirect reference to Genesis 3:15. This view has some scholarly support, but the Greek text does not say *child* (as in Christ) but *children*.

4. Women will be saved (preserved from obscurity and corruption) by bearing and raising children. A woman will often find her greatest satisfaction and meaning in life not by seeking the male role but in fulfilling God's design for her life as a wife and mother. This does not mean, however, that she cannot be engaged and find a measure of fulfillment outside the home (Proverbs 31). This last interpretation seems to be the best choice, although it is also somewhat problematic.

Lesson 5: Definition of Spiritual Maturity

1. a. In the immediate context the phrase simply emphasizes the importance of what is about to be said. The use of the statement does not imply degrees of biblical inspiration. Paul meant that what he was about to say should not be overlooked. Unfortunately, even though Paul added emphasis, this teaching point has still been missed by many Christians.
   b. "A good work."

2. "Must be".

3. 1. Christian women are to quietly receive Bible instruction in the churches (1 Timothy 2:11). The word *quiet* (Gk. *hesuchia*) does not mean complete silence or not talking. The word is used in Acts 22:2 and 2 Thessalonians 3:12 to mean "settled down, undisturbed and not unruly." A different Greek word (*sigao*) means to be silent or say nothing.
   2. Christian women are not allowed to teach men (1 Timothy 2:12).
   3. Christian women should not assume a position of spiritual leadership (1 Timothy 2:12; **not ... have authority over a man**).
   4. The plain reading of the passage dealing with the scriptural qualifications for pastor/teachers indicates that the word *man* is not used generically but specifically to identify the masculine gender (1 Timothy 3:1–7; the differentiation between men and women is not foreign to the passage, 1 Timothy 2:8–9; 3:11–12).
   5. One of the qualifications for pastor/teacher is that he must be able to manage his own house well—a biblical responsibility given to the man (1 Corinthians 11:3; Ephesians 5:22–24). Note: The Greek text offers one additional reason why women should not serve in the

office of pastor/teacher. The Greek adjectives describing the spiritual qualifications for the pastor/teacher are all in the masculine gender.

4. a. The spiritual qualities for pastoral leadership appear to form an excellent composite profile of spiritual maturity and address the believer's need for control over his own spirit, his relationship with others (including his own family), and his personal testimony to the world. The believer should remember, however, that the consistent demonstration of these spiritual qualities will only be manifested through his life as he walks in the Spirit (Galatians 5:22–24). Attempting to produce any list of spiritual responsibilities without focusing on Christ will inevitably lead to a form of legalism.
   b. Answers will vary.

5. 1. Temperate: It means to be free from influences that cloud the believer's thinking. The Greek word (*nephalios*) was used in classical Greek to mean "not mixed with wine." The overseer must be a spiritually alert thinker, balanced in his understanding and not diverted by false teaching.
   2. Sober-minded: The Greek word (Gk. sophrona) means self-controlled, sober (but not somber), earnest, sound. The overseer should be balanced in his judgments so that he fulfills his God-ordained ministry and relegates pleasure and hobbies to their proper place. The overseer must never be thought of as the church clown.
   3. Of good behavior: The Greek word (*kosmios*) is the same word that is translated "modestly" in 1 Timothy 2:9. It means well ordered, organized. The word not only refers to the structure of his teaching but also to the various aspects of his life. The ministry is no place for the man whose life is a continual presentation of chaos and unfulfilled responsibilities.

6. a. The phrase means one against whom it is impossible to bring a charge of wrongdoing that withstands the test of impartial judgment. It does not mean free from accusation or allegation, because no man is immune from the threat of false witness.
   b. He should not be considered for the office of pastor because he might become conceited when others look to him for spiritual advice and counsel. He might also fall into the condemnation incurred by the devil.

c. Satan is a created being (generally believed to be an archangel who came under the judgment of God due to his prideful rebellion; Isaiah 14:12–15). Motivated by pride, Satan rebelled against God and experienced His judgment. A young Christian who is placed in the office of pastor/teacher before he is ready can be overcome by pride and incur judgment from God.

7. While some support can be offered for each of the views listed, the construction of the Greek phrase (literally—a one-woman man) seems to favor the last interpretation. The spiritual leaders of the church (both pastors and deacons) should be men who are committed to meeting the various spiritual, emotional, and physical needs of their wives. According to this view, there should be no hint of flirtatious behavior in the life of the spiritual leader. All spiritual leaders should be "one-woman" men.

8. If the elder or pastor/teacher is not able to lead his home effectively, he does not qualify to lead the church (1 Timothy 3:5). The pastor's leadership of his home is a good indication of his ability to lead Christians within a local church. Note: There are several other practical reasons why it is important for a pastor to have a good home life:
   1. The families in the church will often look to the pastor and his family as an example to follow.
   2. If the pastor's family is in disarray, the people in the church will probably not seek his counsel on family problems.
   3. If the pastor is not leading his family in a manner glorifying to the Lord, he will be largely ineffective when he teaches on family issues. This will open the door to spiritual attack on the families in the church.

   Other answers could apply.

9. a. 1. He should understand his role as a pastor and commit himself to fulfilling his responsibilities before God.
      2. He should communicate his responsibility to the church and his family.
      3. He should spend quality time with his wife and children, seeking to understand their various needs and loving them for who they are, not just because they will be an asset to the ministry.
      4. He should pray for himself, his wife, and his family and teach them how to live for God. Many pastors have overlooked the spiritual

needs of their own families.

5. He should strive to understand the doctrine of God's sovereignty so that he is able to do his best and leave the results to God.
6. He should strive to maintain good personal Bible study habits so that his heart is filled with the love of God.
7. He should understand that if he fails his family, he does not qualify to serve in the pastoral office.
8. He should not overburden his wife and family with spiritual responsibilities that God has given to the entire church. Other answers could apply.

b. 1. Pray for them daily, asking God to give them grace, wisdom, and protection.
2. Support them and not expect them to do all the work.
3. Be patient with them and their families, realizing that they have a difficult calling in life.
4. Don't expect the elders' wives to be church staff just because the pastors are servants of the Lord and the church.
5. Grant the pastors' children the right to mature physically, emotionally, and spiritually at a normal rate. Other answers could apply.

Lesson 6: Servants of God and His Church

1. "Likewise." Just as the elder or pastor/teacher must meet certain spiritual and practical qualifications, the deacon must also meet certain qualifications. **The deacon must be ...**

2. a. 1. Both should be men of careful, balanced thinking (pastor: **blameless, sober-minded** [1 Timothy 3:2]; deacon: **reverent** [1 Timothy 3:8]).
2. Both should be men who are not in bondage to things that waste their time and turn them away from the work of the Lord (pastor: **not given to wine** [1 Timothy 3:3]; deacon: "not … addicted to much wine" [1 Timothy 3:8 NASB]).
3. Both are to be free from the love of money (**not greedy for money**; 1 Timothy 3:3, 8). .
4. Both are to place a high priority on the leadership of their families (1 Timothy 3:4–5, 12).
5. Both are to be tested before they serve in their respective offices

(pastor--his family [1 Timothy 3:4–5]; deacon—his character and faithfulness in service [1 Timothy 3:10]).

b. 1. The pastor has the extra qualification of being able to teach (1 Timothy 3:2).

2. There is additional emphasis on the quality of gentleness for the pastor (1 Timothy 3:3).

3. a. The Greek word (*semnous*) means worthy of respect, dignified. It denotes a seriousness of thinking and character. It includes a recognition that the fulfillment of life's responsibilities has implications beyond the immediate. The word does not convey the idea of a somber disposition.

b. The routine ministrations of the deacon would regularly make him knowledgeable about the personal affairs of certain individuals and families within the church (a family crisis, financial need, etc.). The need to be discreet with privileged information is essential to promote unity within the church and to protect the privacy of the people in the church. The phrase also addresses the need for the deacon to be consistent with what he says. A deacon who wanted to simply please people might be tempted to say one thing to one person and something quite different to another. A deacon who did this would quickly lose spiritual credibility.

4. 1. Overdue bills. 2. An unwillingness to financially support the work of the Lord. 3. Excessive use of credit. 4. A grudging spirit about giving to the Lord. 5. Disharmony and disputes over money within the marriage relationship. 6. Impulse spending. 7. Jealousies and envy of others who have more financially. 8. Overcommitment to work. Other answers could apply.

5. 1. The men of the church were to be tested for a period of time to see if they possessed the spiritual qualifications necessary to serve in this important ministry.

2. Paul told Timothy to let them serve if they were beyond reproach. This seems to indicate that Timothy had the additional responsibility of not allowing individuals to serve if they did not meet the qualifications.

6. A deacon has the opportunity to be a great spiritual encouragement to

other believers in the church (1 Timothy 3:13, **obtain for themselves a good standing**). They also gain great confidence in the faith as they are given special opportunities to serve the Lord (1 Timothy 3:13).

7. A third group within the church that is similar in many ways to the office of deacon. The use of the word *likewise* indicates that a third distinct group is in view. However, the absence of the feminine form of the word *deacon* (Romans 16:1, conspicuously absent in this passage) mitigates against the deaconess view. A careful examination of the particular ministry of these women (1 Timothy 3:11; Titus 2:3) indicates that certain qualified Christian women held a unique ministry within the early church. The fact that they ministered to the younger women in the church seems to imply that they were generally older women who fulfilled this distinct ministry.

8. a. He wrote to instruct Timothy how to administrate the church according to God's will.
   b. He described the church as the house of God, the church of the living God, and the pillar and ground of the truth. The house of God emphasizes the close spiritual family bond that should exist within the church and the pillar and ground of the truth emphasizes the need for the church to be God's faithful witness of the truth.

9. a. Paul said the time would come when the people in the church would not endure sound doctrine but, **according to their own desires, because they** [had] **itching ears**, they would **heap up for themselves teachers; and they will turn their ears away from the truth, and be turned aside to fables.**
   b. Answers will vary, but could include pray more diligently, preach the Word, and equip believers for active ministry in their place of influence (workplaces, neighborhoods, etc.)

10. Jesus Christ.

Lesson 7: Doctrines of Demons

1. a. Savage wolves.
   b. The false teachers would attack the church and draw away disciples after themselves. They would do this by speaking perverse things (Gk.

diastrepho—distort, turn away), which means they would teach subtle heresies that sound right but turn God's people away from the truth.

2. a. Some believers will depart or fall away from the faith.
   b. They accepted (**giving heed to**) false doctrine (**deceiving spirits and doctrines of devils**).

3. The two phrases, **deceiving spirits and doctrines of demons**, likely refer to one kind of false teaching. The first phrase likely refers to the effects or results of the false teaching and the second refers to the demonic source of the teaching. False teaching always leads believers away from the truth. The second phrase (**doctrines of demons**) means that the false teachings are advanced by Satan and his demons rather than doctrines about demons (demonology).

4. The Bible likely identifies them as **deceiving spirits and doctrines of demons** (1) to highlight the true source or origin of all false teaching and (2) to emphasize the danger of false teaching. Many believers are too accepting of false doctrines and appear to view false doctrine as merely a matter of personal interpretation of the Word.

5. a. 1. They are hypocrites. 2. They teach man-made doctrines as truth.
   b. Throughout the history of the church, there has been a long list of religious groups that have repeated this error—Judaizers, Gnostics, Seventh-Day Adventists, etc. Scripture endorses fasting (Acts 14:23) and warns against gluttony (Deuteronomy 21:20; Proverbs 23:21), but it doesn't endorse the concept that believers should be mandated by a church to abstain from eating certain types of foods for the purpose of spiritual sanctification. The apostle Paul called this practice demonic.

6. a. Answers will vary.
   b. Answers will vary, but a believer should separate from a false teacher who is morally or ethically corrupt for two reasons: (1) The believer could easily be deceived and start believing false doctrine, and (2) the believer who continues to listen gives tacit endorsement to someone who needs to repent of his sin.

7. a. 1. Marriage is honorable (Hebrews 13:4).

2. Every creature that God has created is to be used by God's people (1 Timothy 4:3). Note: This assumes that the things God has created are also used for the specific purpose He intended.
3. Everything God has created is good (1 Timothy 4:4).
4. Nothing that God created **is to be refused if it is received with thanksgiving** (1 Timothy 4:4).

b. **With thanksgiving** means believers should be grateful for God's abundant provision of physical nourishment. The second phrase (**sanctified by the word of God and prayer**) means that whatever the believer eats has been set apart by God for his nourishment, and he should recognize this as he partakes. Realizing this, the believer should accept this as a great safeguard against license or abuse of a God-given privilege. Interestingly Paul said, **Whether you *eat* or *drink*, or whatever you do, do all *to the glory of God*** (1 Corinthians10:31, emphasis added). Some Bible scholars believe that this entire process (receiving God's provision and eating in a manner glorifying to God) is consecrated by the believer when he prays in sincerity before the meal. Man should eat to live and not live to eat.

8. God allows false teachers to exist to test His people to see whether they love Him (Deuteronomy 13:1–3). Those believers who love God also love His Word and they will discern whether the teaching they receive is from God or not.

Lesson 8: Walk the Talk

1. a. 1. Timothy was to faithfully instruct the church in the things of God (1 Timothy 4:6).
2. Timothy was to do what he taught others (1 Timothy 4:6–7)
3. Timothy was to reject (not listen to and tell others not to listen) to fables and other teachings that were mere religious speculations (1 Timothy 4:7)

b. The word *minister* means servant and it could be appropriately applied to all believers, since Jesus has called every believer to be His servant (Mark 9:35).

2. a. Believers should **exercise** [themselves] **toward godliness** (NIV: "train yourself to be godly"). The Living Bible (a paraphrase) reads, "Spend

your time and energy in the exercise of keeping spiritually fit." This naturally means that a believer should be in the Word and pray every day, asking God to reveal Himself through the Word, confessing sin, and seeking to know and walk with God more closely.

b. Answers will vary.

3. True godliness means being conformed to the image and likeness of Christ, which is accomplished through an abiding relationship with Jesus Christ and the Holy Spirit. Being religious, on the other hand, is commonly understood to mean conforming to a religious standard or code of conduct that focuses on external adherence or compliance. The first is focused upon a living and dynamic relationship, and the second is focused on external religious dictates.

4. Paul realized that godliness is profitable for all people and impacts them both now and for all eternity.

5. The Potential-actual view. Jesus Christ's death on the cross paid the price for man's sin debt (John 19:30; Gk. *tetelestai*—to finish, complete; used as a Greek commercial term equivalent to "paid in full"). However, only those who have accepted Christ's substitutionary death possess the gift of eternal life. The word "specially" (Gk. *malista*—especially, specifically, most of all; a superlative form of the Greek adverb *mala*—very) emphasizes that the salvation offered to all men has specifically been applied to those who are saved. Note: The Temporal-eternal view is worthy of some consideration, but the predominant use of the Greek root for Savior *(sozo)* is eternal redemption. The author is not familiar with any NT reference that uses this Greek word in two different ways in a single verse.

6. a. 1. He was to communicate the Word of God with a degree of authority (1 Timothy 4:11, **command**: Gk. *paraggello*—command, order, charge, prescribe).
   2. He was to faithfully teach the Word of God (1 Timothy 4:11; the word translated *teach* is a Greek present tense, which indicates continuous action.).
   3. He was to maintain a good personal testimony (1 Timothy 4:12).

   b. 1. His speech (in word).
   2. His conduct (in conduct).

3. His relationship to others (in love).
4. His personal walk with God (in spirit).
5. His faith in God (in faith).
6. His private commitment to maintain mental and moral purity (in purity).

7. a. 1. He was to have the Scriptures read publicly to the church.
   2. He was to encourage or exhort the church to obey the Word of God.
   3. He was to patiently and diligently teach the Word of God.
   b. Paul emphasized the word of God in his preaching and teaching so that his listeners would place their faith in Jesus Christ rather than in the wisdom of man (1 Corinthians 2:5).

8. Timothy was to exercise his spiritual gift (**not neglect the** [spiritual] **gift**; 1 Timothy 4:14) because the proper use of the gift would help him mature spiritually (1 Timothy 4:15). Paul might also be implying that Timothy's spiritual progress would be a spiritual encouragement to the church.

9. If Timothy pursued godliness and was diligent in his teaching, both he and the church would be rescued from the spiritual danger of false teachers (1 Timothy 1:3–4; 4:1–3) and his own theological error that naturally comes as a result of spiritual complacency. In this context the word *salvation* (Gk. *sozo*—to save, heal, keep safe and sound, rescue from danger) cannot mean spiritual salvation because man does not save himself or others. Earlier in the letter, Paul acknowledged Timothy's faith in Christ (1 Timothy 1:2). In Paul's first letter to the Corinthians, Paul said he lived a godly life so that he might save some (1 Corinthians 9:19–22). He was saying that his dedication to the Lord added credibility to the gospel of Jesus Christ; not that he could redeem another man's soul.

Lesson 9: Care and Correction

1. a 1. Older men as fathers. 2. Younger men as brothers. 3. Older women as mothers. 4. Younger women as sisters.
   b. Answers will vary.

2. The Word of God should be preached with God's authority so the listeners understand the importance of applying the truth to their lives. The Word

of God should be ministered privately to individuals with sensitivity and gentleness so that they do not feel that they are being talked down to or berated. Both the public and private ministration of the Word should be presented with a loyalty to the truth and love for people (Ephesians 4:15).

3. The pastor's relationship to the younger women in the church should be conspicuously free of any hint of impropriety or indiscretion.

4. The Greek verb *timao* is related to the English noun *time* and primarily means "price" or "value" and then "honor" or "reverence." In this context the meaning of the word **honor** appears to be "give an appropriate financial compensation." It is important to understand that the financial help is not simply a gift. It is remuneration for a Christian service rendered. In a widow's case, it was her faithful prayers and the good deeds she did for others during her lifetime. The English word *honorarium* helps us understand the inclusion of the monetary element in the word *honor*.

5. a. Her immediate family.
   b. 1. He has denied the faith.
      2. He was worse than an infidel or unbeliever.
   c. Even unbelievers recognize the need to care for the physical needs of their own (Matthew 5:43–47). God's people are regularly taught to fulfill their family responsibilities. If a Christian refuses to meet his family responsibilities, he is worse than an unbeliever (in this particular situation) because he has a greater knowledge and accountability to God (James 4:17).

6. The applicant (in this case, widows) must first look to her family for financial assistance before she looks to the church. Moreover, she must meet a stringent test before she receives assistance from the church. Conversely, many government welfare programs are lax in their qualification process and seldom require applicants to look to their families for financial assistance. This failure causes at least two problems: (1) it fosters irresponsible financial decision-making and forsakes fiscal accountability within the family structure, and (2) it makes indebtedness to the point of the need of welfare relatively painless, knowing that financial assistance is easy to come by and the consequences of unwise financial decision-making are minimized.

7. It appears that the Ephesian church (and perhaps other early NT churches) had a formal list of widows who had previously made a formal vow or pledge to serve the Lord following the death of their husbands. The pledge likely included a commitment not to remarry and to serve the Lord faithfully. If they remained faithful to their pledge and fulfilled the requirements for financial assistance, they could appeal to the church for financial support at age sixty. Younger widows, who had made this pledge (Gk. *pistis*, which may indicate "solemn promise" or "oath"), but later decided to remarry, had broken their vows. The breaking of a vow to God would naturally cause them to incur God's condemnation (Ecclesiastes 5:4).

8. While the context indicates that financial remuneration is involved, it is impossible to determine the exact meaning of this unique phrase. The major views and some brief considerations:
   1. The Honor and honorarium View. This view believes that certain pastors or elders should receive respect (honor) and financial compensation (honorarium) for their faithful service. However, it also means that some elders or pastors should receive respect but no compensation—a rather unlikely arrangement and one inconsistent with Scripture (1 Timothy 5:18).
   2. The Double-the-widow View. This view believes that the elders should receive twice the financial support that the widows receive. Although the context (the way the word **honor** is used in verse 3, etc.) seems to add credibility to this view, a literal application of this interpretation seems illogical. A pastor who served well and had a large family would only receive twice as much as an elderly woman.
   3. The Generosity View. This view holds that the **double honor** refers to the church's need to be generous with those pastors or elders who faithfully fulfill (work hard at) their ministerial responsibilities, especially in preaching and teaching. In this view the double honor would include an extra measure of respect and the appropriate remuneration, without fixing a specific financial amount. As different social and family situations would naturally influence this spiritual responsibility of the church, the need to establish a general principle becomes obvious. This last view appears to be the best interpretation.

9. a. The pastors or elders. The entire context (1 Timothy 5:17–25) is addressing the spiritual leaders of the church. The context is also

dealing with the administration of these spiritual leaders within the local church. The emphasis in the verse is also on the continuation of sinful behavior. While this specific passage is addressing the leaders, it is also true that any Christian who persists in willful rebellion against God exposes himself to church discipline (Matthew 18:15–17).

b. The entire church assembly. The most natural understanding of the phrase *rebuke before all* (Gk. *enopion panton*) would be the entire church. A pastor's ministry within the church is a matter of congregational (public) concern. If a pastor continues to sin for a period of time, the need for rebuke, confession, and spiritual restoration becomes apparent. The public rebuke will serve as a warning to the church that not even pastors or elders are exempt from discipline (1 Timothy 5:20). Note: Nothing is said in the passage about the exact nature of the sin or whether the offense disqualified the elder from future spiritual leadership.

10. a. These believers who were present when the overseers confronted the leaders who were sinning would fear that the same could happen to them. This would naturally have a remedial and purifying impact and effect in their lives. The believers would likely examine their own hearts to see if there were areas of secret sin in their lives. They would likely confess any sin in their lives and gain a new respect for the Word of God and the overseers of the church who are willing to minister to the people without partiality.

b. The true character of a believer will eventually be revealed. In the case of some Christians, their spiritual maturity is readily apparent; for others, it is not. Therefore, the spiritual character of an individual must be observed for a time before he is endorsed. Timothy should not endorse others too quickly. If Timothy endorsed a man who was not ready for the ministry and the man later proved to be incompetent, Timothy would share the responsibility for the man's ineffective ministry. If overseers are careful to select men who are scripturally qualified, the need for future disciplinary action is greatly reduced.

Lesson 10: The Good Fight of Faith

1. a. 1. The name of God would be spoken against or reviled (Gk. *blasphemeo*).
      2. The doctrine (teaching about God) of the church would be mocked or disparaged by unbelievers who observed the disrespect the Christians showed their unsaved employers. Although it is not stated that the masters are unsaved in 1 Timothy 6:1, the comparison with the masters in 1 Timothy 6:2 substantiates this interpretation.
   b. Answers will vary.

2. a. 1. 1 Timothy 1:3–7: These false teachers were likely Jewish legalists who (1) taught fables as truth, (2) placed unwarranted credence on (Jewish) genealogies, and (3) misinterpreted and misapplied the Old Testament Law of Moses (Mosaic Law, Law, Old Covenant) and made it mandatory for all Christians to obey.
      2. 1 Timothy 4:1–4: These false teachers were likely of Gnostic origin since their main teaching was ascetic in nature (forbidding to marry and abstaining from certain foods).
   b. Proud, knowing nothing, obsessed with disputes and arguments over words which result in envy, strife, reviling, evil suspicions, and useless wranglings. Men of corrupt minds, destitute of the truth, and men who use religion for gain.

3. They have corrupt minds and are destitute of the truth. They believe that religion (**godliness**) is a means of great (personal) gain for themselves. Their focus was on personal financial gain rather than serving God.

4. True godliness is a great benefit (**great gain**) to the individual because it allows him or her to experience an inner contentment that material possessions will never give. The Greek word *autarkeia* (from *autos*—self and *arkeo*—suffice, content) signifies an inner satisfaction that is independent of outward circumstances. When believers come to this point in their spiritual life, they have indeed found something special.

5. 1. A Christian cannot take his material possessions with him when he dies (1 Timothy 6:7).

2. Material possessions will never bring lasting peace and happiness (Ecclesiastes 2:11, 17).
3. Every man's material accomplishments will be forgotten shortly after his death (Ecclesiastes 2:16).
4. All men must eventually relinquish control of everything they own to someone else (Ecclesiastes 2:21).
5. A Christian will not be able to serve God effectively if he becomes mentally and physically consumedwith financial advancement (2 Timothy 2:4).

6. Not as long as he or she serves the Lord and sincerely dedicates his or her life and business to God. There are several individuals in Scripture who possessed substantial material wealth (Abraham, Job, Barnabas) or had significant positions in society (Joseph, Daniel, Luke) who were also greatly used by God. They used their position and resources for righteous purposes. The problem is not the amount of money an individual possesses, but the individual's attitude toward it.

7. a. The love of money that is really the desire or lust for financial gain.
   b. 1. Man falls into temptation (1 Timothy 6:9).
      2. Man falls into a snare (1 Timothy 6:9).
      3. Man falls into many foolish and hurtful lusts (1 Timothy 6:9).
      4. Man can be drowned in destruction and perdition (1 Timothy 6:9).
      5. Believers can stray from the faith (1 Timothy 6:10).
      6. They can pierce themselves with many sorrows (1 Timothy 6:10).

8. a. 1. Satan is constantly trying to trap the believer into trusting in riches rather than in God.
      2. The use of this particular word emphasizes the believer's need to take specific steps to avoid this temptation.
      3. The use of the word *flee* emphasizes the reality of the spiritual danger that the Christian faces.
      4. The use of this word emphasizes the Christian's inability to resist this temptation if he does not flee.

      Other answers could apply.
   b. 1. He was to fight the good fight of faith, which means that he was to trust God for his material needs rather than himself (1 Timothy 6:12). It also means that he was not to succumb to temptation.

2. He was to grow in his relationship with Christ and allow it to be the focus of his devotion (**lay hold of eternal life**; 1 Timothy 6:12).
3. He was to live a holy and pure Christian life until death or the appearing of Jesus Christ (1 Timothy 6:14).

c. Answers will vary.

9. 1. He gives life to all things (1 Timothy 6:13).
   2. He is the only Potentate (sovereign), the King of kings and the Lord of lords (1 Timothy 6:15).
   3. He alone possesses immortality (1 Timothy 6:16).
   4. He dwells in unapproachable light that no man has seen or can see (1 Timothy 6:16).
   5. He is worthy of all honor (1 Timothy 6:16).
   6. He possesses everlasting power (1 Timothy 6:16). This means His power (to rule, to save) will never diminish.

10. a. 1. They can be tempted to be proud, thinking they acquired their material wealth without God's help.
       2. They can be tempted to trust in their material possessions rather than in God and His provision.
    b. Answers will vary.

11. Timothy was to guard himself and the church against doctrinal error. In order to do this he would have to be diligent to avoid meaningless and worldly conversation that would waste his time. He would have to be alert to the subtle infiltration of doctrinal errors that subverted the true teaching about the person and work of Christ (Gnosticism).

12. Answers will vary.

Final Exam

Every person will eventually stand before God in judgment—the final exam. The Bible says, ***And it is appointed for men to die once, but after this the judgment*** (Hebrews 9:27).

May I ask you a question? *If you died today, do you know for certain you would go to heaven?* I did not ask if you're religious or a church member, nor did I ask if you've had some encounter with God—a meaningful spiritual experience. I didn't even ask if you believe in God or angels or if you're trying to live a good life. The question I *am* asking is this: *If you died today, do you know for certain you would go to heaven?*

When you die, you will stand alone before God in judgment. You'll either be saved for all eternity, or you will be separated from God for all eternity in what the Bible calls the lake of fire (Romans 14:12; Revelation 20:11–15). Tragically, many religious people who believe in God are not going to be accepted by Him when they die.

> ***Many will say to Me in that day, "Lord, Lord, have we not prophesied in Your name, cast out demons in Your name, and done many wonders in Your name?" And then I will declare to them, "I never knew you; depart from Me, you who practice lawlessness!"*** (Matthew 7:22–23)

God loves you and wants you to go to heaven (John 3:16; 2 Peter 3:9). If you are not sure where you'll spend eternity, you are not prepared to meet God. God wants you to know for certain that you will go to heaven.

> ***Behold, now is the accepted time; behold, now is the day of salvation.*** (2 Corinthians 6:2)

The words ***behold*** and ***now*** are repeated because God wants you to know that you can be saved today. You do not need to hear those terrible words, ***Depart from Me ....*** Isn't that great news?

Jesus himself said, ***You must be born again*** (John 3:7). These aren't the words of a pastor, a church, or a particular denomination. They're the words of Jesus Christ himself. You *must* be born again (saved from eternal damnation) before you die; otherwise, it will be too late when you die! You can know for certain today that God will accept you into heaven when you die.

These things I have written to you who believe in the name of the Son of God, that you may* know *that you have eternal life.

(1 John 5:13)

The phrase ***you may know*** means that you can know for certain before you die that you will go to heaven. To be born again, you must understand and accept four essential spiritual truths. These truths are right from the Bible, so you know you can trust them—they are not man-made religious traditions. Now, let's consider these four essential spiritual truths.

Essential Spiritual Truth

#1

The Bible teaches that you are a sinner and separated from God.

No one is righteous in God's eyes. To be righteous means to be totally without sin, not even a single act.

There is none righteous, no, not one;
There is none who understands;
There is none who seeks after God.
They have all turned aside;
They have together become unprofitable;
There is none who does good, no, not one.
(Romans 3:10–12)

...for all have sinned and fall short of the glory of God.
(Romans 3:23)

Look at the words God uses to show that all men are sinners—**none, not one, all turned aside, not one**. God is making a point: all of us are sinners. No one is good (perfectly without sin) in His sight. The reason is sin.

Have you ever lied, lusted, hated someone, stolen anything, or taken God's name in vain, even once? These are all sins.

Are you willing to admit to God that you are a sinner? If so, then tell Him right now you have sinned. You can say the words in your heart or aloud—it doesn't matter which—but be honest with God. Now check the box if you have just admitted you are a sinner.

❒ God, I admit I am a sinner in Your eyes.

Now, let's look at the second essential spiritual truth.

Essential Spiritual Truth

#2

The Bible teaches that you cannot save yourself or earn your way to heaven.

Man's sin is a very serious problem in the eyes of God. Your sin separates you from God, both now and for all eternity—unless you are born again.

For the wages of sin is death.
(Romans 6:23)

And you He made alive, who were dead in trespasses and sins.
(Ephesians 2:1)

Wages are a payment a person earns by what he or she has done. Your sin has earned you the wages of death, which means separation from God. If you die never having been born again, you will be separated from God after death.

You cannot save yourself or purchase your entrance into heaven. The Bible says that man is **not redeemed with corruptible things, like silver or gold** (1 Peter 1:18). If you owned all the money in the world, you still could not buy your entrance into heaven. Neither can you buy your way into heaven with good works.

> ***For by grace you have been saved through faith, and that not of yourselves; it is the gift of God, not of works, lest anyone should boast.*** (Ephesians 2:8–9)

The Bible says salvation is **not of yourselves**. It is **not of works, lest anyone should boast**. Salvation from eternal judgment cannot be earned by doing good works; it is a gift of God. There is nothing you can do to purchase your way into heaven because you are already unrighteous in God's eyes.

If you understand you cannot save yourself, then tell God right now that you are a sinner, separated from Him, and you cannot save yourself. Check the box below if you have just done that.

❒ God, I admit that I am separated from You because of my sin. I realize that I cannot save myself.

Now, let's look at the third essential spiritual truth.

Essential Spiritual Truth

#3

The Bible teaches that Jesus Christ died on the cross to pay the complete penalty for your sin and to purchase a place in heaven for you.

Jesus Christ, the sinless Son of God, lived a perfect life, died on the cross, and rose from the dead to pay the penalty for your sin and purchase a place in heaven for you. He died on the cross on your behalf, in your place, as your substitute, so you do not have to go to hell. Jesus Christ is the only acceptable substitute for your sin.

For He [God, the Father] made Him [Jesus] who knew [committed] no sin to be sin for us, that we might become the righteousness of God in Him.
(2 Corinthians 5:21)

I [Jesus] am the way, the truth, and the life. No one comes to the Father except through Me.
(John 14:6)

Nor is there salvation in any other, for there is no other name under heaven given among men by which we must be saved.
(Acts 4:12)

Jesus Christ is your only hope and means of salvation. Because you are a sinner, you cannot pay for your sins, but Jesus paid the penalty for your sins by dying on the cross in your place. Friend, there is salvation in no one else—not angels, not some religious leader, not even your religious good works. No religious act such as baptism, confirmation, or joining a church can save you. There is no other way, no other name that can save you. Only Jesus Christ can save you. You must be saved by accepting Jesus Christ's substitutionary sacrifice for your sins, or you will be lost forever.

Do you see clearly that Jesus Christ is the only way to God in heaven? If you understand this truth, tell God that you understand, and check the box below.

❒ God, I understand that Jesus Christ died to pay the penalty for my sin. I understand that His death on the cross was the only acceptable sacrifice for my sin.

Essential Spiritual Truth

#4

By faith, you must trust in Jesus Christ alone for eternal life and call upon Him to be your Savior and Lord.

Many religious people admit they have sinned. They believe Jesus Christ died for the sins of the world, but they are not saved. Why? Thousands of moral, religious people have never completely placed their faith in Jesus Christ *alone* for eternal life. They think they must believe in Jesus Christ as a real person and do good works to earn their way to heaven. They are not trusting Jesus Christ alone. To be saved, you must trust in Jesus Christ *alone* for eternal life. Look what the Bible teaches about trusting Jesus Christ alone for salvation.

> ***Believe on the Lord Jesus Christ, and you will be saved.***
> (Acts 16:31)
>
> ***...that if you confess with your mouth the Lord Jesus and* believe *in your heart that God has raised Him from the dead, you will be saved. For with the heart one believes unto righteousness, and with the mouth confession is made unto salvation.... For there is no distinction between Jew and Greek, for the same Lord over all is rich to all who call upon Him. For "whoever calls on the name of the Lord shall be saved.***
> (Romans 10:9–10, 12–13)

Do you see what God is saying? To be saved or born again, you must trust Jesus Christ *alone* for eternal life. Jesus Christ paid for your complete salvation. Jesus said, **It is finished!** (John 19:30). Jesus paid for your salvation completely when He shed His blood on the cross for your sin.

If you believe that God resurrected Jesus Christ (proving God's acceptance of Jesus as a worthy sacrifice for man's sin) and you are willing to confess Jesus Christ as your Savior and Lord (master of your life), you will be saved.

Friend, right now God is offering you the greatest gift in the world. God wants to give you the *gift* of eternal life, the *gift* of His complete forgiveness for all your sins, and the *gift* of His unconditional acceptance into heaven when you die. Will you accept His free gift now, right where you are?

Are you unsure how to receive the gift of eternal life? Let me help you. Do you remember that I said you needed to understand and accept four essential spiritual truths? First, you admitted you are a sinner. Second, you admitted you were separated from God because of your sin and you could not save yourself. Third, you realized that Jesus Christ is the only way to heaven—no other name can save you.

Now, you must trust that Jesus Christ died once and for all to save your lost soul. Just take God at His word—He will not lie to you! This is the kind of simple faith you need to be saved. If you would like to be saved right now, right where you are, offer this prayer of simple faith to God. Remember, the words must come from your heart.

> **God, I am a sinner and deserve to go to hell. Thank You, Jesus, for dying on the cross for me and for purchasing a place in heaven for me. I believe You are the Son of God and You are able to save me right now. Please forgive me for my sin and take me to heaven when I die. I invite You into my life as Savior and Lord, and I trust You alone for eternal life. Thank You for giving me the gift of eternal life. Amen.**

If, in the best way you know how, you trusted Jesus Christ alone to save you, then God just saved you. He said in His Holy Word, ***But as many as received Him, to them He gave the right to become the children of God*** (John 1:12). It's that simple. God just gave you the gift of eternal life by faith. You have just been born again, according to the Bible.

You will not come into eternal judgment, and you will not perish in the lake of fire—you are saved forever! Read this verse carefully and let it sink into your heart.

> ***Most assuredly, I say to you, he who hears My word and believes in Him who sent Me has everlasting life, and shall not come into judgment, but has passed from death into life.***
> (John 5:24)

Now, let me ask you a few more questions.

According to God's holy Word (John 5:24), not your feelings, what kind of life did God just give you? ______________________________

What two words did God say at the beginning of the verse to assure you that He is not lying to you? ____________ ____________________

Are you going to come into eternal judgment? ❐ YES ❐ NO

Have you passed from spiritual death into life? ❐ YES ❐ NO

Friend, you've just been born again. You just became a child of God.

To help you grow in your new Christian life, we would like to send you some Bible study materials. To receive these helpful materials free of charge, e-mail your request to **info@LamplightersUSA.org.**

Appendix

Level 1 (Basic Training) Student Workbook

To begin, familiarize yourself with the Lamplighters' *Leadership Training and Development Process* (see graphic on page 112). Notice there are two circles: a smaller, inner circle and a larger, outer circle. The inner circle shows the sequence of weekly meetings beginning with an Open House, followed by an 8–14 week study, and concluding with a clear presentation of the gospel (Final Exam). The outer circle shows the sequence of the Intentional Discipleship training process (Leading Studies, Training Leaders, Multiplying Groups). As participants are transformed by God's Word, they're invited into a discipleship training process that equips them in every aspect of the intentional disciple-making ministry.

The Level 1 training (Basic Training) is *free*, and the training focuses on two key aspects of the training: 1) how to prepare a life-changing Bible study (ST-A-R-T) and 2) how to lead a life-changing Bible study (10 commandments). The training takes approximately 60 minutes to complete, and you complete it as an individual or collectively as a small group (preferred method) by inserting an extra week between the Final Exam and the Open House.

To begin your training, go to www.LamplightersUSA.org to register yourself or your group. A Lamplighters' Certified Trainer will guide you through the entire Level 1 training process. After you have completed the training, you can review as many times as you like.

When you have completed the Level 1 training, please consider completing the Level 2 (Advanced) training. Level 2 training will equip you to reach more people for Christ by learning how to train new leaders and by showing you how to multiply groups. You can register for additional training at www.LamplightersUSA.org.

Intentional Discipleship

Training & Development Process

Multiplying Groups

The 5 Steps of Faith for Starting Studies

Training Library

Online Resources

Leading Studies

ST-A-R-T

10 Commandments

Solving All Group Problems

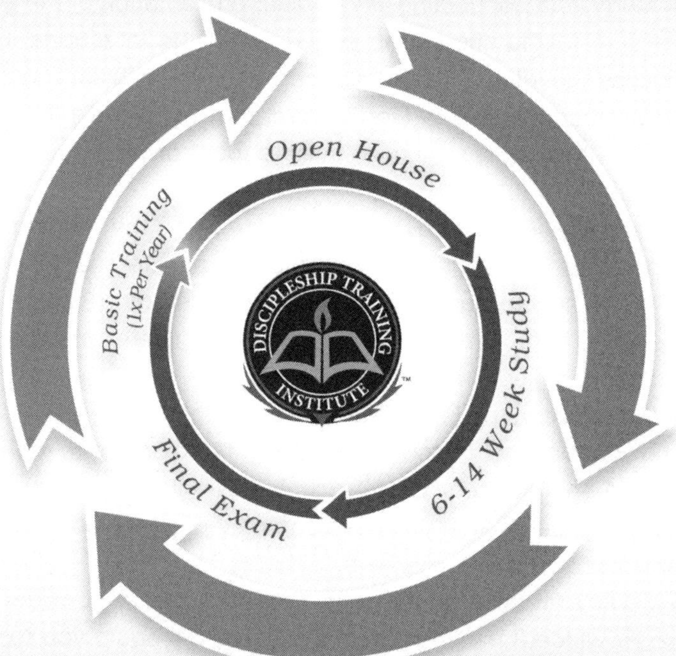

Training Leaders

4 Responsibilities of a Trainer

Leadership Training

4 Levels of Student Development

3 Diagnostic Questions

John A. Stewart © 2017

How to Prepare a Life-Changing Bible Study

ST-A-R-T

Step 1: ______________________ and ______________________.

Pray specifically for the group members and yourself as you study God's Word. Ask God (____________________) to give each group member a rich time of personal Bible study, and thank (____________) God for giving you a desire to invest in the spiritual advancement of each other.

Step 2: ______________ the ______________________.

Answer the questions in the weekly lessons without looking at the ______________ ____________.

Step 3: ______________and ______________________.

Review the Leader's Guide, and ________ every truth you missed when you originally did your lesson. Record the answers you missed with a ________ ____________ so you'll know what you missed.

Step 4: ______________ ______________.

Calculate the specific amount of time ________ __________ to spend on each question and write the start time next to each one in the ____________ using a ______________________.

How to Lead a Life-Changing Bible Study

10 COMMANDMENTS

1	2	3
4	5	6
7	8	9
	10	

Lamplighters' 10 Commandments are proven small group leadership principles that have been used successfully to train hundreds of believers to lead life-changing, intentional discipleship Bible studies.

Essential Principles for Leading Intentional Discipleship Bible Studies

1. The 1st Commandment: The ______________________ Rule.

   The Leader-Trainer should be in the room _____ minutes before the class begins.

2. The 2nd Commandment: The _________-_____ Rule.

   Train the group that it is okay to ____________, but they should never be __________________.

3. The 3rd Commandment: The _______________________ Rule.

   ________________, _________________, ________________ ask for ______________ to ______ the ________, ______, and ___________ the questions. The Leader-Trainer, however, should always _______ the questions to control the ________ of the study.

4. The 4th Commandment: The ____:____ Rule.

   ________ the Bible study on time and ______________ the study on time ______________ _________________. No exceptions!

5. The 5th Commandment: The _____________ Rule.

   Train the group participants to _______________ on God's Word for answers to life's questions.

1	2	3
4 59:59	5	6
7	8	9
	10	

6. The 6th Commandment: The ________________ Rule.
   Deliberately and progressively ____________ _____ participants into the group discussion over a period of time.

7. The 7th Commandment: The _________ __________ Rule.
   ___________ the participants to get _________ the answers to the questions, not just _________ or ___________ ones.

8. The 8th Commandment: The ____________________ Rule.
   ________________ the group discussion so you __________ the lesson _____ _________ and give each question __________________ ___________.

9. The 9th Commandment: The _____-_________________ Rule.
   Don't let the group members talk about ______________ ________________, ______________ __________________________, or _____________________ _________________.

10. The 10th Commandment: The ______________________ Rule.
    _____________ God to change lives, including _____________.

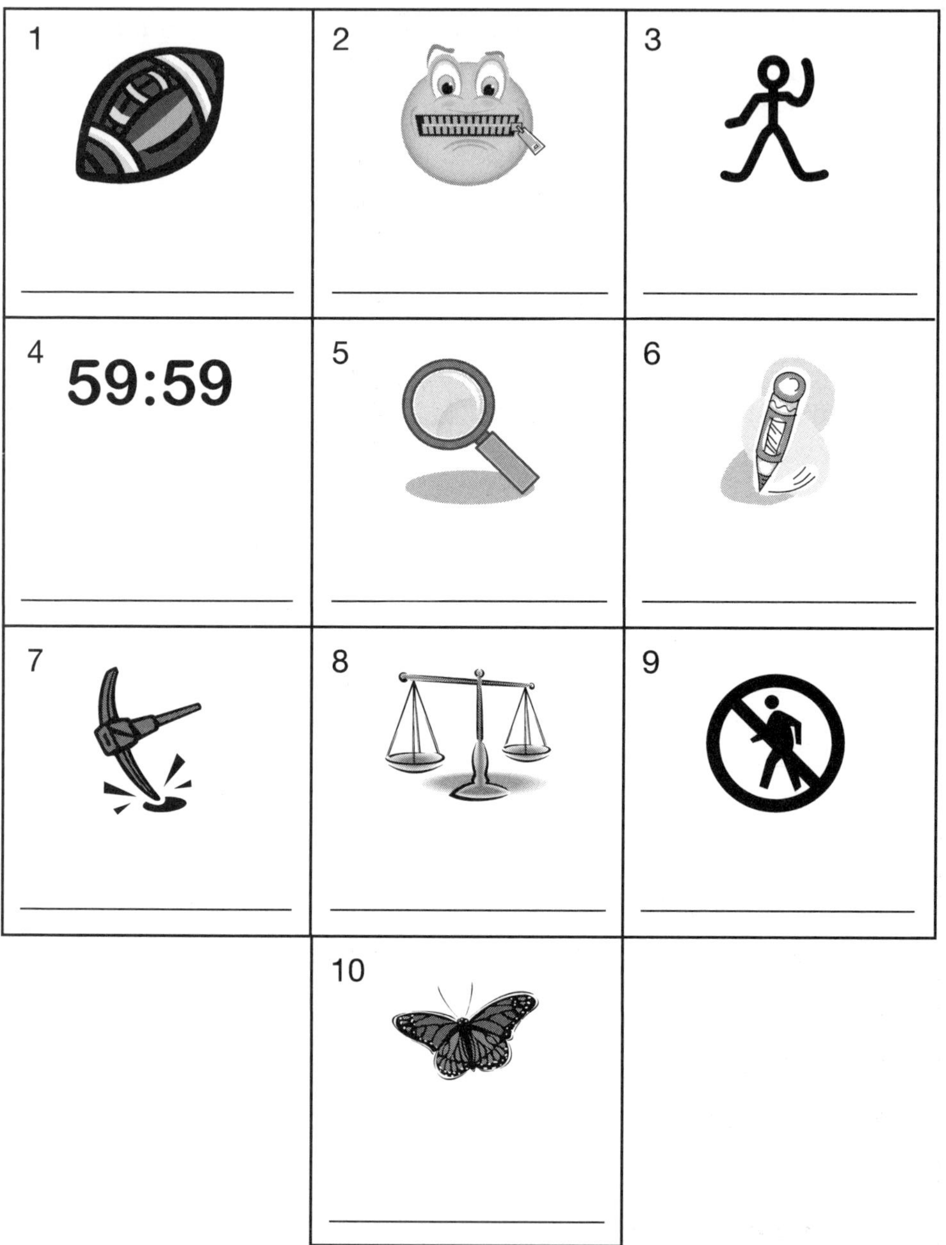
1
2
3
4
59:59
5
6
7
8
9
10

Choose your next study from any of the following titles

- John 1-11
- John 12-21
- Acts 1-12
- Acts 13-28
- Romans 1-8
- Romans 9-16
- Galatians
- Ephesians
- Philippians
- Colossians
- 1 & 2 Thessalonians
- 1 Timothy
- 2 Timothy
- Titus/Philemon
- Hebrews
- James
- 1 Peter
- 2 Peter/Jude

Additional Bible studies and sample lessons are available online.

For audio introductions on all Bible studies, visit us online at www.Lamplightersusa.org.

Looking to begin a new group?
The Lamplighters Starter Kit includes:

- 8 James Bible Study Guides
  (students purchase their own books)
- 25 Welcome Booklets
- 25 Table Tents
- 25 Bible Book Locator Bookmarks
- 50 Final Exam Tracts
- 50 Invitation Cards

For a current listing of live and online discipleship training events, or to register for discipleship training, go to www.LamplightersUSA.org/training.

Become a Certified Disciple-Maker or Trainer

Discipleship Training Institute

Certificate of Completion

This is to certify that ____________________

has successfully completed the requirements of the

____________________ course.

Date | President

Training Courses Available:

- Leader-Trainer
- Discipleship Coach
- Discipleship Director
- Certified Trainer (Level 1)

Contact the Discipleship Training Institute for more information (800-507-9516).

The Discipleship Training Institute is a ministry of Lamplighters International.